Praying the Story

Praying the Story

the

Story

Pastoral Prayers from the Psalms

Maxie Dunnam
John David Walt, Jr.

ABINGDON PRESS / *Nashville*

PRAYING THE STORY
PASTORAL PRAYERS FROM THE PSALMS

Copyright © 2005 by Abingdon Press

All rights reserved.

This book is printed on acid-free paper.

Library of Congress Cataloging-in-Publication Data

Dunnam, Maxie D.
  Praying the story : pastoral prayers from the Psalms / Maxie Dunnam and John David Walt, Jr.
    p. cm.
  ISBN 0-687-34316-X (pbk. : alk. paper)
  1. Prayer—Christianity. 2. Bible. O.T. Psalms—Liturgical use. 3. Pastoral prayers. I. Walt, John David. II. Title.

  BV226.D86 2005
  264'.1—dc22

                                                    2005000690

05 06 07 08 09 10 11 12 13 14—10 9 8 7 6 5 4 3 2 1
MANUFACTURED IN THE UNITED STATES OF AMERICA

To our mothers and fathers, who taught us the story and how to pray.

Contents

Introduction

Invocation

The word "prayer" stands for a radical interruption of the vicious chain of interlocking dependencies leading to violence and war and for an entering into a totally new dwelling place. It points to a new way of speaking, a new way of breathing, a new way of being together, a new way of knowing, yes, a whole new way of living. . . .

Prayer is the center of the Christian life. *It is the only necessary thing.* (Luke 10:42)

—Henri J. M. Nouwen, "Prayer and Peacemaking,"
The Only Necessary Thing: Living a Prayerful Life,
New York: Crossroad Publishing Co., 1999, p. 25.

Stories create worlds. The world we construct in worship determines the world we inhabit with our lives. The story we remember in our gatherings determines the future we imagine for our lives.

A third grade teacher gave a creative writing assignment to her class. "I'm going to begin a story and your task is to write a creative and imaginative ending. There was once an ant and a grasshopper. The ant worked hard all summer, storing up food for the winter. The grasshopper played all summer and did no work. Winter came and the grasshopper, starving to death, went to the ant's house. 'Mr. Ant, my family and I have no food and we will not last through the winter. You have plenty for your family and enough for us. Would you share?' Now write the ending." One of the little boys, Mark, shot his hand into the air. "Yes, Mark," responded the teacher. "Can I draw a picture instead of writing the ending?" "Yes, Mark," she replied, "You may draw a picture, but you *must* also write the ending."

The papers came streaming in. As always, a few papers proffered this sad ending: "So the ant said, 'No! Mr. Grasshopper. There's only enough food for me and my family. You don't deserve any food. You should have worked in the summer.' And the grasshopper died." Most of the papers, however, came in with the traditional ending that I call "God likes it when we share." It goes, as you recall, "So the ant shared his food with the grasshopper and they all lived happily ever after." But there was one more paper. Remember Mark, the kid who wanted to draw a picture? When his paper came in, the teacher, visibly disturbed, proceeded to call his mother. She recounted the assignment, saying, "In my fifteen years of teaching this class and giving this assignment, I have never seen this ending." Here's how Mark finished the story: "So the ant gave all his food to the grasshopper. And the ant died." And underneath the ending he had drawn a picture of three crosses.

Out of a child's living memory of the story of God came the pure and unbridled imagination of the kingdom of heaven. In every era, the people of God author endings to the story of God. We live in an age in which one hundred million children live on the streets, many of them orphaned. HIV/AIDS ravages the African continent at unprecedented rates. Broken sexuality threatens to destroy the very fabric of our society. Unthinkable genocide brews in the Sudan while hurricanes wreak devastating losses on untold thousands for whom recovery will take decades.

Corporate Prayer Catalyzes

This book encourages us to remember *God's* story as we pray. Prayer is the furnace in which memory kindles into the conflagration of kingdom imagination; in which the mind descends into the heart, illuminating the mission of God in the world. Corporate prayer catalyzes the lives of your congregants; it sharpens the mission of the church. As saints throughout the ages have declared, *prayer isn't preparation for the battle; prayer is the battle.*

Prayer isn't preparation for the battle; prayer is the battle.

The Church Is the School of Prayer

As pastors ourselves, we know the dilemma of unrelenting demands on your time. Although we hope that this book will stretch your experience of prayer, we have uniquely designed it to inspire you with ready-to-use resources to use in worship. We offer a new vision of an ancient practice—reaching into the past for the sake of the present.

Our hope as you use these prayers is for the church to recover her vocation as a school of prayer. For better or worse, from infants upward, people learn prayer in church. Would that our words spoken in prayer begin to eclipse our words spoken about prayer. When they do, our amen will ring with exultant exclamation!

Learning to Pray the Story

On a visit to our seminary, a Native North American friend remembered for us a hunting story from his childhood. As he and his father trekked deeper and deeper into the forest, he became afraid they were lost. Every few moments his father would stop and look around, carefully studying the surroundings but deliberately looking back in the direction from which they came. After this had gone on a while, the son asked his father if they were lost. His father answered, "No, Son, we are not lost. So not to get lost I have spent twice as much time paying attention to where we have been as to where we are going." In this same way, worship is a narrative journey of remembering into the future. The essence of remembering is paying attention to the journey along which one has traveled. The failure to remember inevitably leads to a deep sense of lostness and disorientation.

Pastoral prayer implicitly functions as a narrative plot device. In prayer, the people of God don't so much tell a story as they get inside of one: "One of the remarkable qualities of the story is that it creates space. We can dwell in a story, walk around, find our own place. The story confronts but does not oppress; the story inspires but does not manipulate. The story invites us to an encounter, a dialog, a mutual sharing.... The story brings us into touch with the vision and so guides us" (Henri J. M. Nouwen, *The Living Reminder:*

Service and Prayer in Memory of Jesus Christ [New York: Seabury Press, 1977], 65-66).

Blues Clues, the imaginative children's cartoon, unfolds the interplay of Joe, a real live person, and Blue, a cartoon world dog. Joe is real, not animated; however, Joe lives with Blue in the world of animation. Each episode includes an almost liturgical pattern of songs, games, and crafts revolving around Joe's task of pursuing Blue's clues to solve a mystery. As though it weren't enough for Joe to enter Blue's world, it gets deeper. With ritualistic consistency at a certain point in each episode, Blue pauses to study a hanging picture on the wall. Next, she jumps through the frame and into the picture. Joe responds, "Blue skadood. We can too!" He follows Blue, jumping through the frame where the two find themselves completely surrounded by the moving scenes of the world of the picture. Be it in an African safari or a journey into the inner city, Blue and Joe have effectively skadood out of their world and into the imaginative world of the story. They are inhabiting the story.

Prayer as Story Convergence

When prayer is textured with the memory of the story, those praying seamlessly skadoo into the imaginative possibilities of God's world. The pastoral prayer as narrative plot device skadoos the church into the abiding current of God's mind, heart, and will. Prayer, when well crafted, remembers the story, engages and locates people through the naming of their needs, joins individual persons into a journeying people by interceding for the mission of the church, and imagines the kingdom of God in all of its glorious fulfillment. Prayer, when spiritually led, gathers up participation into embodied expression. When the church prays, she offers up her life to the triune God in such ways that the story of God unfolds into new chapters of the church's life. Through our praying, we inhabit the story of God. Prayer narrates people into a story. But what story?

We're often called to our intercessions. We pray for the hungry. God responds, "I will answer your prayer. What will you do for the hungry?" We pray for the lonely, and God says, "I hear you. What will you be for the lonely?" We pray for peace in the world, and God answers, "Peace is my dream, and peace begins with you. How will you be a peacemaker?"

In corporate prayer—an intercessory prayer offered for the whole gathered people—four primary strands of story converge: theological, personal, ecclesial, and eschatological. The theological strand signifies the grand setting of the Scriptures, the vision that God has for us. The personal dimension points to the multiple stories of individual people gathered for worship, touching on felt needs and pressing situations. The ecclesial dimension identifies the story of the church and its healing mission in the world. The eschatological dimension articulates the end, redemption, and resolution of the story, focusing on the consummation of God's kingdom on earth as it is in heaven.

Scriptural Pastoral Prayer Is Theological

Interspersed throughout the prayers of the 150 psalms, the psalmist continually harkens memory to the larger context of the narrative of God's activity in their midst. The people of God dwell within the ever-expanding storied journey from Creation to New Creation, from Exodus to New Exodus, from the first Adam to the second Adam, and from Exile to Homecoming.

The psalmist consistently unfolds the ongoing saga of God's people inside the expansive story of the mighty deeds of God in history. Note, for instance, how many times the Creation, Exodus, Red Sea, and Sinai events get remembered throughout the Psalms. The central movement of canonical praying is remembering, for in the biblical scheme of things the past is the key to the future.

Praying from the story navigates us into the future. Some of the newest vehicles being produced today come equipped with sophisticated navigational equipment. A small computer screen shines like a beacon in the center of the dashboard. And it talks. It's called a Global Positioning System, the most cutting-edge vehicular technology available. All the driver has to do is enter in the desired destination. As the journey begins, a visual map and written instructions appear on the screen indicating landmarks, turns, and exact distances in between. If that weren't enough, a voice calls out directions audibly as the turns approach.

As Jesus fasted and prayed for forty days in the wilderness, a reality similar to Global Positioning System emerged, with Satan tempting and enticing Jesus at every turn. At every opportunity to make a wrong turn, which would have been fatal to his mission of salvation, a similar type of navigational device activated within Jesus: the story of God. God's word, through the means of the unfolding story, was deeply etched into Jesus' memory, and when Jesus was confronted with temptation, it naturally surfaced with navigational accuracy through the words, "It is written...." As Jesus remembered Israel's wandering in the wilderness, God's word to Israel reemerged in his praying imagination, empowering him to journey creatively where Israel had failed. I suspect, the Gospel writers captured in this wilderness temptation narrative a consistent practice in Jesus' life, the practice of praying the story.

In similar fashion, the church continues to journey with Jesus, first in prayerful imagination and then in active demonstration as we live out the epic story of God in our age. Prayer becomes a powerful point of entry into the story, a narrative act of participation, a way of rehearsing our part in the drama of salvation for the sake of the world.

Pastoral Prayer Is Personal

Prayer must move from the larger story to engage people in their present experience. Ranging from mountaintop joys to valleys of despair, authentic prayer emerges only from real life. From the birth of babies to battles with cancer, ranging from dating to divorce, delight to depression, and somewhere between happy and hopeless, pastoral prayer identifies with persons at defined junctures of need and joins their heart's cry to God. The central movement of personal prayer is need-naming. People come to church for many reasons, but one remains constant: a deep need for help. On any given Sunday, families whose lives are being torn apart are present in worship. They celebrate births and grieve deaths. Difficult decisions seek discerning guidance, while lost opportunities require hope-filled comfort. Prayer, more specifically the pastoral prayer, unveils the vital signs of the worshiping congregation.

O LORD, you have searched me and you know me. You know when I sit and when I rise; you perceive my thoughts from afar. You discern my going out and my lying down; you are familiar with all my ways. (Psalm 139:1-3 NIV)

6

Perhaps the most significant part of many of the psalms may not actually be part of the Psalms at all. It is those two small words found just beneath the number and just above the first verse. The two words are "Of David." Seemingly insignificant at first glance, the two words contain the stuff of incarnation; the Word made flesh and dwelling among us. "Of David" shows these lyrical poems are not the poetic musings of philosophical pondering. Quite the opposite is true. The simple words "Of David" are the gut-wrenching, heart-rending, spirit-lifting cries of a real person with a real life in the real world. Our storied lives become woven into the Psalms as we insert our name in the blank after "of." The most critical leap for the student of the Psalms comes when those small authenticating words "of David" become "of John David" or "of Maxie" (*Heart of Worship Files 2*, ed. by Matt Redman [Ventura, CA: Regal Books, 2003]).

The psalmist cries out, "O God, you are my God, earnestly I seek you; my soul thirsts for you, my body longs for you, in a dry and weary land where there is no water" (Psalm 63:1 NIV).

We must learn a way of prayer both implicitly personal and explicitly communal. The church proffers a thousand definitions for the practice of prayer. Although useful, many of our notions of prayer are far too individualistic in scope. Prayer, by nature, is personal, but Christian prayer is never individualistic. When we pray, "Our Father," we express personal intimacy and yet a radical inclusiveness of others. Too often, our prayers settle for an easy existentialism. In other words, we reduce prayer to a coping device to help us appropriate the peace of God in our warring circumstances. As a result, we speak too readily of the power of prayer and too little of the power of God.

Pastoral Prayer Is Ecclesial

Ecclesial means of or relating to the church. Pastoral prayer runs the circuit from individuated persons and their particular needs to a people, the people of God, fashioning them together into a movement in mission to all the world. The ecclesial dimension of prayer reminds the church of her crucial intercessory position between a longing God and a lost world. Nothing constitutes the church for the sake of the world like her prayers do. The central aim of ecclesial prayer is missional intercession. So the psalmist called us to, "Pray for the peace of Jerusalem: 'May those who love you be secure. May there be peace within your walls and security within your citadels.' For the sake of my brothers and friends, I will say, 'Peace be within you' " (Psalm 122:6-8 NIV).

The psalmist continually reveals the longings of a people on pilgrimage, a descriptive word about the nature of the church. "Blessed are those who dwell in your house; they are ever praising you. Blessed are those whose strength is in you, who have set their hearts on pilgrimage" (Psalm 84:4-5 NIV).

Prayer declares the intersection of heaven and earth, more specifically: *On earth as it is in heaven.* I vividly remember a trip to the former Soviet Union in the early 1990s.

> Until November 1989, every church in Czechoslovakia was severely restricted by the Communist government. Christians could not evangelize. They had to be careful how they spoke in public.... No sign could be erected outside their churches. They could make no public declarations. They could not even ring their church bells.
>
> Then in November 1989, a group of students confronted a group of young soldiers, and that catalyst brought the revolution against the government out in the open and to full flower. Everybody took to the streets, and the old Communist regime knew that it was over.
>
> Christians there told us the story. It was decided that on November 27 at noon, everybody in the country would walk out of homes, businesses, offices, factories, or fields. Everybody would simply walk out into the streets at noon. Every bell in every church in Czechoslovakia would be rung at noon. And when that day and time came, bells that had been silent for forty-five years began to ring. It was electric. Everybody knew that something new had come.
>
> Dr. Vilem Schneeberger, one of the pastors, said that for the first time they were able to put a sign out in the front of their church in Prague. On the sign were written four words: "The Lamb Has Won." (Maxie Dunnam, *This Is Christianity* [Nashville: Abingdon Press, 1994], 138)

Pastoral Prayer Is Eschatological

Finally, the eschatological dimension of pastoral prayer focuses the church's praying imagination on the kingdom of God as it will finally come. "It is the whole vision of an Eschaton that is now missing outside the church. The assembly of believers must therefore itself be the event in which we may behold what is to come" (Robert W. Jenson, "How the World Lost Its Story" in *The New Religious Humanist,* ed. Gregory Wolfe [New York: Free Press, 1997], 146-47).

As time began with Creation, so will it end with the consummation of the New Creation. The eschaton must increasingly shape the church's longing and clarify her prayers. Here we celebrate the ultimate reconciliation of the world with God, on earth as it is in heaven, when every nation, tribe, and tongue will gather before the throne and worship the Lamb. The central dimension of eschatological prayer is imagining. "Let heaven and earth praise him, the seas and all that move in them, for God will save Zion and rebuild the cities of Judah. The people will settle there and possess it; the children of his servants will inherit it, and those who love his name will dwell there" (Psalm 69:34-36 NIV).

"If, in the *post*-modern world, a congregation ... wants to be 'relevant,' its [services] must be unabashedly events of shared apocalyptic vision. 'Going to church' must be a journey to the place where we will behold our destiny, where we will see what is to come of us" (Jenson, "How the World Lost Its Story," p. 147).

> Then I looked, and I heard the voice of many angels surrounding the throne and the living creatures and the elders; they numbered myriads of myriads and thousands of thousands, singing with full voice, "Worthy is the Lamb that was slaughtered to receive power and wealth and wisdom and might and honor and glory and blessing!" (Revelation 5:11-12)

Jenson challenges that the church's services must again become a place of "seeing," where "beatific vision is anticipated and trained."

East Side Baptist Church is a little country church in Perry County, Mississippi. It is the church in which I, Maxie, was converted under the preaching of Brother Wiley Grisson, a fifth-grade-educated pastor who preached the gospel with power. The church is about 200 yards up the hill from our old home. Behind it is a cemetery where I'll be buried someday.

Dad and Mom—whom in my adult life I affectionately called "Mutt" and "Co-bell"—are buried there. Co-bell died five years ago, and Mutt three years ago. I still miss them. On Co-bell's tombstone are the last words she spoke to Mutt, "I'll see you." On his tombstone is his response as he held her hands as she died, "I'll be there"—a great witness to their confidence in eternal life and heaven as our home. Unstudied and unplanned, it is the aliveness of imagination, giving expression to the promise of eschatological hope, about which John wrote:

> Then I saw a new heaven and a new earth; for the first heaven and the first earth had passed away, and the sea was no more. And I saw the holy city, the new Jerusalem, coming down out of heaven from God, prepared as a bride adorned for her husband. And I heard a loud voice from the throne saying, "See, the home of God is among mortals. He will dwell with them; they will be his peoples, and God himself will be with them; he will wipe every tear from their eyes. Death will be no more; mourning and crying and pain will be no more, for the first things have passed away." And the one who was seated on the throne said, "See, I am making all things new." (Revelation 21:1-5*a*)

I was with Co-bell and Mutt when the exchange recorded on their tombstones took place. Three of their five children were with them that night. We prayed and cried, recalled some funny stories, but mostly we sang. We sang of the hope that is ours beyond death, and we sang in the reassurance of southern country gospel music, songs like

> When we all get to heaven,
> What a day of rejoicing that will be!
> When we all see Jesus,
> We'll sing and shout the victory!

That's the chorus. One of the stanzas goes:

> Sing the wondrous love of Jesus;
> Sing his mercy and his grace.
> In the mansions bright and blessed
> He'll prepare for us a place. (Eliza E. Hewitt, "When We All Get to Heaven," *The United Methodist Hymnal* [Nashville: The United Methodist Publishing House, 1989])

Our praying, like our singing, recalled that story we know and expressed the wild gamut of feelings among us. Something akin to all those feelings of joy in the presence of sadness, anticipation, and hope in the presence of death must characterize our corporate worship, especially our praying.

Praying the Story

Even These Dark Days ...

On the morning of September 11, 2001, our seminary community raced into Estes Chapel. We jettisoned the planned worship for the morning, opting instead for an extended season of prayer. The Psalms located us before God: "God is our refuge and strength, a very present help in trouble. Therefore we will not fear, though the earth should change, though the mountains shake in the heart of the sea; though its waters roar and foam, though the mountains tremble with its tumult" (Psalm 46:1-3). Our praying led us to remember the story of Jeremiah and the tragic destruction of the Temple, the defining structure of God's people. Rising up from our deep place of mourning and sadness came perhaps the centerpiece of biblical prayer in God's word to Jeremiah: "See, I am the LORD, the God of all flesh; is anything too hard for me?" (Jeremiah 32:27).

These dark days marked a turning point in the shared prayer journey of our seminary community. Despite fluctuating intensity in the days since September 11, our intentionality in the practice of pastoral prayer keeps climbing to new heights. Through thoughtful remembering, intentional posturing, and expressive liturgy, we continue to learn new dimensions of corporate prayer. As we stumble and stretch for the vision, we see worship transforming from a resting place for the weary to a missional gathering of monumental proportions. Through prayer, we believe God is narrating us more deeply into the story of salvation.

From tiny rural congregations to massive megachurches, pastors everywhere long for renewal. Throughout history, renewal most often happens as a result of reformation in worship. Recent decades chronicle "wars" over competing styles of worship. Although fresh forms of contemporary worship help capture the longing of the church and provide much needed refreshment, this comes up short of real renewal. Our insatiable appetite for the presence of God in worship and the kingdom of heaven on earth cries out for more.

In this book, we contend the reformation most needed in worship today involves not so much style, but story, a shift of focus from what we are doing to what God has done. What big story unfolds in our worship? How does the story reveal God and define the identity of people? And how does our being together narrate us into that story? We believe prayer captures the central dimension of worship.

Embodying Prayer Through Posture

Corporate prayer offered by the pastor can so often be a disconnected experience in congregational worship. When prayer feels vicarious to parishioners, their hearts easily wander and their minds quickly drift. Though pastoral prayer holds great potential for total engagement, it is too often unrealized. Posturing for prayer uncovers one of the key practices of the people of God in all times and places. Sprinkled throughout the following pages of prayers are creative ideas for developing corporate yet personal posture for prayer. Posture amplifies and enlivens prayer through demonstrating bodily what the prayer seeks to do spiritually.

As a way of growing the church's corporate prayer life, try inviting the congregation to practice intentional posturing for prayer (i.e. kneeling, standing, bowing, open hands) during the pastoral prayer. In each season of the church year, we offer guidance for leading the congregation in this practice. Take a minute prior to the pastoral prayer to teach the people the meaning of a particular posture (such as kneeling for Lent), and invite them to engage in the posture during the prayer to the extent they are able and comfortable in doing so.

Then, at the evening sacrifice, I rose from my self-abasement, with my tunic and cloak torn, and *fell on my knees with my hands spread out* to the LORD my God.

(Ezra 9:5 NIV)

ACTS of Prayer

I need a language that is large enough to maintain continuities and supple enough to express nuances across a lifetime that brackets child and adult experiences, and courageous enough to explore all the countries of sin and salvation, mercy and grace, creation and covenant, anxiety and trust, unbelief and faith that comprise the continental human condition. . . .

Where will we acquire a language that is adequate for these intensities? Where else but in the Psalms? For men and women who are called to leadership in the community of faith, apprenticeship in the Psalms is not an option; it is a mandate. (Eugene H. Peterson, *Working the Angles: The Shape of Pastoral Integrity* [Grand Rapids: Eerdmans Publishing Co., 1987], 39)

It's not at all difficult to identify in scripture the essential elements of prayer. In the Psalms especially, we find the DNA—the building blocks—of prayer. One of the memorable ways that we have identified those elements we call the ACTS of prayer: adoration, confession, thanksgiving, and supplication. Athanasius said that the Psalms were like a gymnasium for all parts of the soul. The design of the DNA of the Psalms is to expose our humanity that we might encounter divinity. What is true of the elements of prayer is reflective of worship in general. One of the great Christian writers of the twentieth century was A. W. Tozer. He had a remarkable way of grappling with some of the deep questions of the Christian life. He was passionate for God, and he described worship as "the missing jewel" in the evangelical church. We're discovering the truth of that—however reticently—these days. Prayer is the primary focus of the believer's life. Corporate prayer is the primary focus of life in the body of Christ.

Adoration

Whether we begin here or not—because praying and worshiping are never a lockstep process—*adoration is a core element of prayer.* David began Psalm 34 with an exultation: "O magnify the LORD with me, and let us exalt his name together" (v. 3). "Magnify" means not to make God big, but to see God as God is. The NIV translates that third verse, "Glorify the LORD with me." When we see God as God is, we glorify him. We "extol" the Lord. We "fear the LORD" (v. 9 NIV). We "taste and see that the LORD is good" (v. 8 NIV). We're confident that when "the righteous cry out . . . the LORD hears them" (v. 17 NIV) and that the Lord "is close to the brokenhearted and saves those who are crushed in spirit" (v. 18 NIV). We are delivered when we "[take] refuge in him" (v. 22 NIV).

Adoration of God is vibrant and dominates our praying as we're captivated with the splendor of God.

The Psalms enable us to pray the story—to see ourselves, to experience ourselves, in the great narrative of God in history and particularly in our personal lives—the story of Creation, the Fall, redemption, and New Creation. Psalm 99 is a good example of this. It's the last in a series of what has been called "enthronement psalms" (Psalms 93, 95–99). These psalms answer the crisis in that nation. The covenant between God and his people had been broken. The king in the line of David had been defeated in battle. In the mind of the people, the defeat of the king was the defeat of God. God's people were crushed and humiliated. The enthronement psalms remind Israel that Moses proclaimed the eternal reign of God long before there was land, long before there was the temple, long before there were kings. So Psalm 99 gets us into the story and is most significant when read alongside Exodus 15, in which Moses proclaimed, "The LORD will reign forever and ever" (v. 18). This was the song that Moses and the Israelites sang after being delivered from Egypt. So Psalm 99 and Exodus 15 are songs celebrating God's reign, and in both God is to be exalted because God is great, awesome, and holy. Thus the fourth book of Psalms (Psalms 90–106) begins with the only psalm attributed to Moses.

Psalm 99, the final climactic enthronement psalm makes specific mention of Moses and Aaron. It also refers to Samuel, who opposed the choosing of a human king because he considered God Israel's only true king. Psalm 89 declares the crisis that exists as a result of the covenant between God and his people having been broken (vv. 38-46), the king in the line of David having been defeated in battle. Psalm 99 assures a later generation, discouraged by these events, that God still reigns. Verses 8 and 9 imply that what God has done in the past, God will continue to do in the present:

> O LORD our God, you answered them;
>   you were a forgiving God to them,
>   but an avenger of their wrongdoings.
> Extol the LORD our God,
>   and worship at his holy mountain;
>   for the LORD our God is holy. (Psalm 99:8-9)

Psalm 99 is like a bridge that reaches from Moses and the events of Exodus 15 to the present day, during which all are called to make a decision as to who reigns and whether we will live under God's rule. "The LORD reigns, let the earth be glad" (Psalm 97:1 NIV). "The LORD reigns, let the [people] tremble" (Psalm 99:1 NIV). The one who reigns is worthy of adoration and praise. This is the first movement of prayer.

There is *power* in adoration and praise. When we remember—even in the midst of adversity—when we consider the work of God in our lives and offer genuine praise for God's blessing, we find new strength and hope in present circumstances. This is seen dramatically in what are called psalms of lament. Many of the psalms fall into this category. There are laments of the community and laments of the individual.

Adoration and praise make one movement in prayer. We adore God for who God is; we praise God for what God is doing.

In both cases, the individual or the community finds themselves suspended between God's promise and the fulfillment of the promise. This is a time when faith is tested. There is no solid proof that God has spoken or that God is in control. These psalms of lament express the distress of the community or the individual at a time of threat when believing that God was with his people is difficult. The following are some sample community laments:

Why do you hide your face?
Why do you forget our affliction and oppression?
For we sink down to the dust; our bodies cling to the
    ground. Rise up, come to our help.
Redeem us for the sake of your steadfast love.
                                          (Psalm 44:24-26)

O God, you have rejected us, broken our defenses;
    you have been angry; now restore us.
You have caused the land to quake;
    you have torn it open; repair the cracks in it,
for it is tottering. (Psalm 60:1-2)

O God, why do you cast us off forever?
Why does your anger smoke against
    the sheep of your pasture? (Psalm 74:1)

Here are samples of individual laments:

Help, O LORD, for there is no longer anyone who is godly;
    the faithful have disappeared from humankind.
They utter lies to each other; with flattering lips
    and a double heart they speak. (Psalm 12:1-2)

My God, my God, why have you forsaken me?
Why are you so far from helping me,
    from the words of my groaning?
O my God, I cry by day,
    but you do not answer;
and by night, but find no rest. (Psalm 22:1-2)

Save me, O God, for the waters have come up to my neck.
I sink in deep mire, where there is no foothold;
I have come into deep waters,
    and the flood sweeps over me.
I am weary with my crying;

> my throat is parched.
> My eyes grow dim with waiting for my God.
>
> (Psalm 69:1-3)

All these psalms lament problems, afflictions, danger, and a deep sense of sin, and the psalmist pleads for God's healing grace. As we study these psalms, we realize that the label "lament" is not altogether right. That word suggests a pessimistic view of life, a morbid concentration on human agony and guilt. This is not the mood of the psalmist even in these psalms of lament. A careful look causes us to know that the psalmist is not concentrating on the distress as such, but is taking his or her distress to the Lord, knowing that the Lord is the judge and at the same time the redeemer. The one to whom the psalmist prays has sovereign power over all distress. God has the power to lift the person out of the "miry bog" and set his or her feet upon a rock (Psalm 40:2). In that sense, the laments are really expressions of praise and hope. The psalmist is praising God even though God is not present. There is *anticipatory* faith. The pray-er believes that although God is absent, he will show his face and deliverance and redemption will come.

We need to learn from the psalmist: adoration and praise move us out of ourselves and our own situation and into the realm of God's grace and power. They take our eyes off our own problems and limitations and enable us to see and receive the limitless resources of the Holy Spirit.

We need to learn from the psalmist: adoration and praise move us out of ourselves and our own situation and into the realm of God's grace and power.

Psalm 103 is one of the most familiar and beloved of all the psalms and is a beautiful illustration of moving out of ourselves and our own situation into the realm of God's grace and power. It begins and ends with a cry: "Bless the LORD, O my soul." The word "bless" (in Hebrew *barak*) originally meant to "bend the knee before"—that is, to bow and offer homage to one's king, one's sovereign.

So, the psalmist brings his whole self—all that he is—to bless God. He knows that his whole life belongs to God and that he is to offer God praise and thanksgiving for God's redemption, healing, lovingkindness, tender mercies, forgiveness, providence, justice, grace, and patience.

The word "all" recurs throughout the psalm. The psalmist does not want to ignore or diminish in any way the completeness of God's grace and compassion. The twenty-two lines of the psalm have been connected to the twenty-two letters of the alphabet, suggesting that the psalmist desires to say it all and labels this the "A to Z" of God's compassion. God rules over all and does all good things for all persons in need; he is to be praised in all places by all creatures with all their being. So the psalmist can but kneel in adoration and praise: "From everlasting to everlasting the LORD's love is with those who fear him" (103:17 NIV).

Confession

The second movement of prayer that we learn from the Psalms is confession. In confession, we examine ourselves and clarify our vision and understanding of who we are in relation to God. This is more than confessing sin, it is honestly locating ourselves before the Lord. It may be like a psalm of lament.

A family has struggled endlessly with the addiction of a family member. The young man has been in and out of treatment. He has been faithful for months and months in his Alcoholics Anonymous community. He has made commitments to the Lord and has sought to follow those commitments, but over and over again he falls. The powerful hands of his addiction drag him down, sometimes to the point of death—in treatment and in jail, over and over again.

The results of a biopsy come. The diagnosis is clear: incurable malignancy, working destructively for months before diagnosis. The doctor says that there are only six to nine months left for this young mother with two children to live.

In both these instances, the young man and the young mom pray; members of the family pray, "Oh, Lord, why did this happen to us? Why did you not intervene and heal? How much more can we take? Our family has been through so much already."

Members of these families are not alone. They complain and cry out to God. David did it. In the first two verses of Psalm 13, he asks the question, "How long?" four times. "How long will you forget me?" "How long will you look the other way?" "How long must I struggle with anguish in my soul?" "How long will the enemy have the upper hand?"

David the psalmist and the family members who cry out in anguish to God because a son is controlled by an addiction or a daughter is diagnosed with a malignancy certain to bring death honestly locate themselves before the Lord. Caught in a "sinking-in-the-swamp" feeling of depression and despair, they tell God precisely how they feel. Not only are they identifying with the cries in Psalm 13, but also they are identifying with Jesus on the cross: "My God, my God, why have you forsaken me?" (Mark 15:34).

In confession, we *locate ourselves honestly before the Lord.* Recently, in the process of moving, I came across some old prayer journals I had kept over twenty years. I was obviously praying the psalms because I found this entry:

> Hear a just cause, O LORD; attend to my cry!
> Give ear to my prayer from lips free of deceit!
> (Psalm 17:1 RSV)

"From Lips Free of Deceit"

> Where are such lips
>   O Lord
> They aren't mine
> Oh, I'm not deliberately deceitful
>   that is—not very often
> But it's very easy *not* to speak
>   to stay quiet when the truth should be spoken
> Easy to stop short of the whole story
>   and leave a distorted image
> Easy to lead the conversation
>   off-track so that the truth will not be pursued.
> Easy to use words with double meanings
>   and put the responsibility of interpreting
>   on someone else.
> Forgive me, Lord.

Lord, I can't say it.
"If thou triest my heart, if thou visitest me by night,
    thou will find no wickedness in me
My mouth *does* transgress."

Forgive me.

Confession locates us honestly before the Lord. We cry out to him because there is no place else to turn. We hope, like the psalmist, we will punctuate our cries of depression and despair with a statement of trust: "But I trust in your unfailing love. I will rejoice because you have rescued me. I will sing to the LORD because he has been so good to me" (Psalm 13:5-6 NLT).

But I trust in your unfailing love. I will rejoice because you have rescued me. I will sing to the LORD because he has been so good to me. (Psalm 13:5-6 NLT)

When we locate ourselves honestly before the Lord, we must center our trust not on the circumstances, but on the character of God. In those circumstances, we pray: "Lord Jesus, I don't feel your presence, so hear my cry of desolation, my anguish and hopelessness. Hear me even though you're absent from me. Hear me and bless me with your presence. Somehow, Lord, use my pain to make me more sensitive to the desperation of persons around me. Also, Lord, use my pain, my desolation, to draw me closer to you. Amen." Our prayer becomes our confession: confession in being honest in locating ourselves before the Lord, but also confession in affirming our faith.

This dynamic becomes transforming in the context of corporate prayer as well as of personal prayer. God is infinitely distant from us because of our sin. When we become aware of this, we become even more aware of the seriousness of our sinfulness. At the same time, because of Christ—his self-giving love, his death as God's gift of himself to us—we know that God is closer to us than even our husband or wife or closest friend. It is not contradictory then to pray to One who is infinitely distant and infinitely near.

Thus God can become our confidant, the One with whom we share—as a son would share with a father, a daughter with her mother, or as we with our closest friends—if we open ourselves up in an ongoing way in intimacy and trust.

What we express corporately must necessarily grow out of and be maintained in solitude.

It's not always easy to remember God and what God has done for us when we're in the midst of desolation, hopelessness, and despair. One of the desert fathers talked about remembrance of God as a profound form of prayer that eventually transforms us and all of our relationships. But that remembrance becomes very difficult in our private praying. It's almost impossible to do this remembering by ourselves. So, we need to pray with others in order that others who know about us and who have walked where we walk can *remember for us* and cultivate memory within us. Healing comes when an intentional community, committed to one another's soul care, affirms one another as lovable and of value to God. Such a relationship enables us to see that our sorrow, sickness, and failings need not define us. The testimony of our friends in the context of mutual caring—their testimony of healing and overcoming—encourages and enriches the one who is presently in despair.

Healing comes when an intentional community, committed to one another's soul care, affirms one another as lovable and of value to God.

The last two verses of Psalm 13 are representative of a pattern that occurs over and over again in the Psalms—a deliberate turning to God and trusting God's unfailing love. "But I trusted in your steadfast love; my heart shall rejoice in your salvation. I will sing to the LORD, because he has dealt bountifully with me" (Psalm 13:5-6). It's a courageous, bold, blatant expression of trust that the circumstances of desolation and despair will not prevail because of who God is. We are helped by those with whom we mutually share to make an affirmation of trust despite the despair we presently feel. "I will sing to the LORD, because he has dealt bountifully with me" (Psalm 13:6). "I will give to the LORD the thanks due to his righteousness, and sing praise to the name of the LORD, the Most High" (Psalm 7:17).

There is also in confession, in locating ourselves honestly before the Lord, the *confession of sin*. This is absolutely essential because our sin separates us from God. Isaiah gave challenging expression to it: "But your iniquities have separated you from your God; your sins have hidden his face from you, so that he will not hear" (Isaiah 59:2 NIV).

Confession is essential because our greatest need is forgiveness. Forgiveness requires repentance and repentance requires confession. Psalm 51 is the Bible's most vivid case. The psalm has been credited to David, who saw what he wanted and took for himself the beautiful wife of Uriah. Another king could have done this without a whisper of blame or guilt—but not David. He had been anointed by God, and he must not sin. Before the story was finished, a murder was committed. When David engineered the setting for Uriah to be killed in battle, adultery and murder brought the guilt that clung to David's blackened soul.

Our greatest need is forgiveness.

What misery and spiritual pain and agony David must have endured until one day the fearless prophet Nathan confronted the king with his tragic condition before a just and holy God. David saw God as the one to whom he must answer.

> Have mercy on me, O God,
>   according to your steadfast love;
> according to your abundant mercy
>   blot out my transgressions.
> Wash me thoroughly from my iniquity,
>   and cleanse me from my sin.
> For I know my transgressions,
>   and my sin is ever before me.
> Against you, you alone, have I sinned,
>   and done what is evil in your sight. (Psalm 51:1-4*a*)

It's interesting that before David mentions his sin, he appeals to God for mercy. It's also interesting that in that moment, he does not dare to say, "My God"; rather, he says, "Have mercy on me, O God." His sin has alienated him from God, so he stands afar off and cries, "O God." To say "my God" would have been the height of presumption.

He uses three words to picture the different aspects of sin. *Pesha* means "rebellion," "transgression"—setting oneself against the will and law of God. It is an act of high treason against the sovereign of the universe. *Awon*, "iniquity," means that which is "twisted" or "warped" or "crooked." It is in reality depravity of conduct. The third word, *hatah*, "sin," means literally "missing the aim or the mark." He recognized the nature of sin—it was something that happened on the inside before it expressed itself outwardly: "Surely you desire truth in the inner parts; you teach me wisdom in the inmost place" (Psalm 51:6 NIV). The verbs he uses indicate that God must do something that David cannot do for himself: blot out, wash me, cleanse me. Only God has the record of his sin and can erase it from the book: *blot out*. His body, mind, and soul have to be dealt with: *wash me thoroughly*. Do whatever it takes to cleanse me completely so that your holy eyes, O God, can be pleased with what you see when you examine me. David is literally sick of sin and wants it all removed by water or by fire or by any other drastic method. He knows what Isaiah was talking about: his iniquities had separated him from God. His sin had caused God's face to be hidden from him—to the point that God might not even hear him.

Still he knows there is a way out for the sinner, so he prays, "Cleanse me with hyssop, and I will be clean; wash me, and I will be whiter than snow" (v. 7 NIV). David knew God better than many of us know God. He knew that nothing was beyond God's infinite power. He gave utterance to a faith in the cleansing touch that could make the vilest sinner clean.

Cleanse me with hyssop, and I will be clean; wash me, and I will be whiter than snow. (Psalm 51:7 NIV)

Faith like this is what makes redemption possible. Confession is the beginning of it. The remedy for our sin begins when we have personally acknowledged our sins and when we have taken responsibility. The accompanying dynamic of repentance is necessary—a genuine sorrow for sin that enables us to turn our backs on sin forever. When that kind of confession and repentance is genuine, forgiveness comes.

And what a joyous forgiveness. Psalm 32 begins: "Happy are those whose transgression is forgiven, whose sin is covered. Happy are those to whom the LORD imputes no iniquity, and in whose spirit there is no deceit" (vv. 1-2).

Sin does not have to separate us from God. God has come to us in Jesus Christ, who is our redeemer. John said, "If we confess our sins, [Jesus] is faithful and just and will forgive us our sins and purify us from all unrighteousness" (1 John 1:9 NIV).

Thanksgiving

Thanksgiving is the third ingredient of prayer that we learn from the psalms. There is a distinction, subtle though it may be, between praise and thanksgiving. We praise God for who he is; we thank him for what he has done and is doing. To be sure, our praise and thanksgiving do get intermeshed, but it is wise and fruitful to be specific in our praise and thanksgiving.

Out of the South from which we both come, there is the wisdom story of the old man who, when asked why he so often talked to himself, replied, "Well, sir, you see, it's this way. I like to talk to an intelligent person, and I like to hear an intelligent person talk." The author of Psalm 103 talked to himself, exerting all the inner powers to stir up gratitude. Few psalms have found their way so completely into the hearts of persons as this favorite of the favorites. No psalm is more beautiful. There is remarkable tenderness here, childlike trust, buoyant hopefulness, and a pure outburst of praise and gratitude that is hardly equaled anywhere in Scripture. Many will have memorized at least the beginning of it from the King James version:

> Bless the LORD, O my soul:
>   and all that is within me,
> bless his holy name.
> Bless the LORD, O my soul,
>   and forget not all his benefits;
> Who forgiveth all thine iniquities;
>   who healeth all thy diseases;
> Who redeemeth thy life from destruction,
>   who crowneth thee with lovingkindness and
>   tender mercies;
> Who satisfieth thy mouth with good things;
>   so that thy youth is renewed like the eagle's.
>   (vv. 1-5 KJV)

The psalmist summons all his faculties and the powers of his whole being to unite in gratitude and praise to God. Søren Kierkegaard expressed it this way:

> It is wonderful how God's love overwhelms us—alas, ultimately I know of no truer prayer than what I pray over and over again, that God will allow me and not be angry with me because I continuously thank him for having done and for doing, yes, and for doing so indescribably much more for me than I ever expected. (*The Prayers of Kierkegaard* [Chicago: University of Chicago Press, 1956], 202)

Kierkegaard takes his cue from the psalmist. The psalmist catalogues six things that God does for His creatures—indescribably much more than we could ever expect. He heals our diseases. He redeems us from destruction. He crowns us with loving-kindness and tender mercies. He satisfies us with good things. He renews our lives like the eagles. The capstone of all of this is the certainty that the Lord is merciful and gracious, slow to anger, and plenteous in mercy (Psalm 103:8). He affirms God's forgiving love in an image that none of us can miss: "As a father has compassion for his children, so the LORD has compassion for those who fear him" (Psalm 103:13). That compassion and love expressed by a parent to a child from God's side is as high as the heavens are above the earth and the extent to which God will go to redeem us is unlimited: "as far as the east is from the west, so far [has] he [removed] our transgressions from us" (v. 12).

As said earlier, there is a connection between praise and thanksgiving. Though there are distinct psalms of praise and psalms of thanksgiving, the psalms of praise anticipate God's deliverance on the basis of an assurance that has been given. Psalms of thanksgiving are praises to God in response to deliverance already experienced. Thus we have the distinction mentioned earlier in that there are two ways of praising God. In one case, we extol God for who God is—his majesty as creator and his mighty works in history. But the hymn of thanksgiving praises God for his action in concrete situations. The individual psalms of thanksgiving were for the most part composed for recitation in the temple as an expression of a person's praise for God's deliverance—for God's concrete intervention, deliverance from distress or illness. In the context of worship, the celebration of a festival, or the worship services in the temple, an individual gave his or her personal testimony to God's saving deeds, and this was seen as a thank offering with praise and thanksgiving coming together. "Enter his gates with thanksgiving, and his courts with praise. Give thanks to him, bless his name" (Psalm 100:4).

Psalm 16 is a wonderful example of thanksgiving. Obviously everything is going right with the psalmist. Though he opens the psalm with a petition, "Keep me safe, O God, for I have come to you for refuge" (v. 1 NLT), he goes on immediately to affirm God's presence in his life. He becomes very specific in his thanksgiving beginning in verse 5: "You alone are my inheritance, my cup of blessing. You guard all that is mine.... I will bless the LORD who guides me; even at night my heart instructs me. I know the LORD is always with me. I will not be shaken, for he is right beside me. No wonder my heart is filled with joy, and my mouth shouts his praises!" (vv. 5, 7-9 NLT).

Keep me safe, O God, for I have come to you for refuge.
(Psalm 16:1 NLT)

The psalmist notes that even at night God is working in his heart to instruct him. Nighttime is a great time to pray—certainly a great time for thanksgiving. The very fact that we have shelter, a bed, a pillow, and covers to keep us warm is enough to stimulate thanksgiving.

But the night watches are also a time for petition and intercession. When we're awakened in the night by a siren, we can pray for persons we know who are in trouble and may be near death. When the telephone wakes us up, we can center on the fact that there are people in the world who do not know the comfort that we know, the security of sleep, and being cared for—and we can pray for them. When we are unable to sleep, we can pray for the well-being of family members, friends, and situations in our community that threaten life.

Psalm 98 is a second example of happy thanksgiving. It is a call to celebrate with joy the righteous reign of God.

Sing to the LORD a new song,
for he has done marvelous things;

his right hand and his holy arm
    have worked salvation for him.
The LORD has made his salvation
    known and revealed his righteousness to the nations.
He has remembered his love and his faithfulness
    to the house of Israel; all the ends of the earth
have seen the salvation of our God. (vv. 1-3 NIV)

Note that the call goes out to the worshiping community at the temple, then to all the peoples of the earth, and to the whole of creation. The great work of salvation is not to be kept quiet. This psalm can't be read silently. It is a large, expansive, joyous psalm read best with corporate voice and the full heart of a celebrating congregation. In this psalm, as much as any place else, the exuberance of Israel's worship is illustrated. People raise their voices in shouts; their praises are chanted and sung, horns are blown, and other musical instruments are played. It may be that God often works quietly, but his great work of salvation is not to be kept quiet—it must be celebrated. So the worshipers sing "a new song, for [the Lord] has done marvelous things." Climactically, the sea, the rivers, and the mountains are invited to join this cosmic song of praise.

Like many of the psalms, Psalm 98 looks backward and forward. The first verses recall Exodus 15 and the mighty saving acts of God as he delivered his people out of Egyptian bondage. He demonstrated his faithfulness to Israel and the covenant he had made to remember them with unfailing love (Psalm 98:3). God the divine warrior had acted for all the world to see. This God of steadfast love who revealed his righteousness to the nations (vv. 2-3) will act in the future as well and will come to rule the world (v. 9).

Here again, we see how the psalms enable us to pray the story. The song of salvation already sung by Moses will continue to be heard and is heard in a triumphant way, as the writer of the book of Revelation declares, "like the roar of a great multitude in heaven shouting: 'Hallelujah! Salvation and glory and power belong to our God'" (Revelation 19:1 NIV).

I have a friend who is a recovering alcoholic and loves country music—especially country gospel. He is a would-be songwriter himself and, in fact, has written some pretty good songs. One of them, which he loves to sing, proclaims what the psalmist was saying here, "O God, we know what you're gonna do because we've seen what you've already done." The story is a continuous one, so the psalmist looks back to a God who has saved, who has delivered, who has been trustworthy, who has demonstrated God's faithfulness, and who proclaims the hope that is ours because the God who has acted in the past will certainly act in the future.

> *In prayer and worship, we're captivated by the splendor of God, and we want to sing a new song unto the Lord.*

In prayer and worship, we're captivated by the splendor of God, and we want to sing a new song unto the Lord. Again, why? The answer: "For the LORD is good and his love endures forever; his faithfulness continues through all generations" (Psalm 100:5 NIV). Psalm 100, from which this affirmation comes, is placed like a book-end at the conclusion of the enthronement psalms and acts as a doxology, a hymn of praise and thanksgiving closing the "God is king" psalms. It underscores the profound truth: to live is to praise God and to praise God is to live.

The reasons for thanksgiving and praise are given. Is there meaning to the fact that the psalmist uses seven (the perfect number) strong, compelling, commandments: "Shout for joy ... worship the Lord ... come before him ... know the Lord who is God made us and we are his ... enter his gates ... give thanks ... praise his name"?

In this doxology, the psalmist makes clear who God is in four key words: goodness, steadfast love, and faithfulness—the essence of God's character.

Supplication

Adoration, confession, and thanksgiving prepare us for *supplication*. Supplication is not a common, everyday word, but it is a powerful one. Paul included it in his instruction for our daily living: "Do not worry about anything, but in everything by prayer and supplication with thanksgiving let your requests be made known to God" (Philippians 4:6).

Supplication is an intense word and combines what we may refer to as petition and intercession in our praying. It is a kind of brooding, longing act of remembrance and hope.

At the heart of prayer and worship is turning our whole being toward God. Sometimes we come with calm and confidence, yet how often do we come with doubts and questions. We bring praise, but also we come in pain. Whether we acknowledge, anger and fear may be in our minds and hearts as much as reverence and awe. We may come to sit still in God's presence, or we may have to wrestle with the angel as Jacob did and refuse to let go until we get a blessing. Supplication is a part of our praying. We are limited for words to express our thanksgiving; but there are times when our feelings are so raw, our concerns so overwhelming, our passion so intense, we can do little more than anguish in the presence of God. We're waiting for the biopsy report of a loved one, or an inexplicable accident drives us to doubt a loving God. A broken friendship leaves us lonely and emotionally distraught.

At the heart of prayer and worship is turning our whole being toward God.

One of the remarkable dimensions of the psalms is the way they can move from crying out for help, to describing their distress in their most straightforward way, then to expressing trust and confidence that God is with them in the midst of their distress. Psalm 69 is a marvelous example of that. The psalmist shares a severe picture of the ridicule and alienation he has experienced in his community—how he has been persecuted because of his relationship and the expression of his relationship to God. He confesses that he is in "deep water, and the floods overwhelm me" (Psalm 69:2 NLT). He says, "I am exhausted from crying for help; my throat is parched and dry. My eyes are swollen with weeping, waiting for my God to help me" (v. 3 NLT). After going on like that, expressing the work of his enemies, the psalmist turns to express confidence that there is aid and comfort, "for your unfailing love is wonderful, ... for your mercy is so plentiful" (v. 16 NLT). "The LORD hears the cries of his needy ones; he does not despise his people who are oppressed" (v. 33 NLT).

We seek the Lord because he can be found. We thirst

because God can and does cool our parched spiritual tongues. We hunger because God offers God's self as the Bread of Life who alone can nourish our famished souls.

In our supplication, we trust God's goodness even when the immediate circumstances of our lives are not good. This ability to trust God's goodness makes us capable of hope, even in a world of hopelessness in which we are involved and engaged.

Our supplication may still have a sense of urgency and anguish about it. We see this in Psalm 71: "O God, don't stay away. My God, please hurry to help me" (v. 12 NLT). He connects his supplication with his stage in life—obviously old in years: "And now, in my old age, don't set me aside. Don't abandon me when my strength is failing" (v. 9 NLT). In our supplication, we struggle with anguish and doubts. Our souls are troubled by the suffering of others, the arrogance of the wealthy, or the way institutions deal oppressively with individuals. We wrestle with questions concerning our mission and ministry, what is right and what is not. As Paul said, we wrestle with principalities and powers. We lay all that out before God, but we know God as the writer of Psalm 71 knew him, as the refuge, the rock, the fortress (vv. 1, 3 NLT).

When we use an acronym such as ACTS as a guide to prayer, it should never be seen as a lockstep way to move in our praying—first adoration, then confession, then thanksgiving, and then supplication. Hardly ever would our praying move in such an ordered pattern, because our praying is an expression of what we're feeling and thinking and hoping and dreaming; our thoughts and our words overlap and stumble over one another and get mixed up together.

Psalm 27 is an example of this. It runs the gamut of emotions: confident praise, deep yearning, fear, desperation—a wide range of emotions all spill out. The juxtaposition of thanksgiving and supplication has caused some scholars to suggest that this psalm is actually two psalms—one of thanksgiving and one of supplication. Whether that is true or not, a deeper wisdom is at work here because the stark opposites unsettle us and cause us to realize that our contradictory mix of feelings can't be denied. So we're challenged to place all our feelings—our yearnings, our fear, our desperation—within the larger context of thanksgiving to God and confidence in the God addressed in the first line of the psalm: "The LORD is my light and my salvation—whom shall I fear?" (Psalm 27:1 NIV).

So why follow thanksgiving with supplication? Sometimes our thanksgiving has to be proleptic—that is, an acknowledgment and a claiming of the "now and not yet." When our supplication follows a thanksgiving that anticipates the "not yet," that trusts, however feebly, that the "not yet" will someday come to be, then our supplication can be honest, yet not bringing us to despair. Even when we do not *feel* thankful, we can *be* thankful because we know that everything is held in the holy hands of the Lord who is our "light and salvation" (Psalm 27:1 NIV). In *supplication,* we hold to all that we are, all that we do, all that we think, and all that we feel; in *thanksgiving,* we release all that we are, all that we do, all that we think, and all that we feel to a God who is faithful and upon whom we can "wait patiently ... [and] be brave and courageous" (27:14 NLT).

The Psalms are identified and labeled in a lot of different ways. In the church's liturgical tradition, which goes back to the Middle Ages, seven psalms were singled out as *penitential* psalms. These psalms are the best examples of supplication that we have in this prayer book of the church. They are called penitential psalms because they express humility before God. The point is made by simply reading verses from each of those seven psalms.

O LORD, do not rebuke me in your anger, or discipline me in your wrath. Be gracious to me, O LORD, for I am languishing; O LORD, heal me, for my bones are shaking with terror. My soul also is struck with terror, while you, O LORD—how long? Turn, O LORD, save my life; deliver me for the sake of your steadfast love. (Psalm 6:1-4)

Happy are those whose transgression is forgiven, whose sin is covered. Happy are those to whom the LORD imputes no iniquity, and in whose spirit there is no deceit. While I kept silence, my body wasted away through my groaning all day long. For day and night your hand was heavy upon me; my strength was dried up as by the heat of summer. Then I acknowledged my sin to you, and I did not hide my iniquity; I said, "I will confess my transgressions to the LORD," and you forgave the guilt of my sin (Psalm 32:1-5)

There is no soundness in my flesh because of your indignation; there is no health in my bones because of my sin. For my iniquities have gone over my head; they weigh like a burden too heavy for me. My wounds grow foul and fester because of my foolishness; I am utterly bowed down and prostrate; all day long I go around mourning. (Psalm 38:3-6)

Create in me a clean heart, O God, and put a new and right spirit within me. Do not cast me away from your presence, and do not take your holy spirit from me. Restore to me the joy of your salvation, and sustain in me a willing spirit. (Psalm 51:10-12)

[We looked at this as the prime example of confession. It also bears the dimensions of supplication.]

For my days pass away like smoke, and my bones burn like a furnace. My heart is stricken and withered like grass; I am too wasted to eat my bread. Because of my loud groaning my bones cling to my skin. I am like an owl of the wilderness, like a little owl of the waste places. I lie awake; I am like a lonely bird on the housetop. (Psalm 102:3-7)

Out of the depths I cry to you, O LORD. Lord, hear my voice! Let your ears be attentive to the voice of my supplications! . . . I wait for the LORD, my soul waits, and in his word I hope; my soul waits for the Lord more than those who watch for the morning, more than those who watch for the morning. (Psalm 130:1-2, 5-6)

Hear my prayer, O LORD; give ear to my supplications in your faithfulness; answer me in your righteousness. Do not enter into judgment with your servant, for no one living is righteous before you. (Psalm 143:1-2)

Let's look specifically in a more expansive way at one of these psalms—the fifth penitential psalm, Psalm 102. It is the prayer of an unnamed individual in great distress. He calls upon God to hear him. He has no one else to whom he might turn. He describes his condition: his days are like smoke (v. 3); his life is like the evening shadow in the grass that withers (v. 11); life is short and suddenly over.

Fever wracks his body, his appetite is gone, and he has lost his ability to sleep. He has been reduced to skin and bones. In a culture in which ill health is understood to be divine punishment for sins, he has been cut off from others. What a pathetic curse he feels: "like an owl among the ruins ... a bird alone on a roof" (vv. 6, 7 NIV). It would be enough to know human rejection; worse is his feeling of divine displeasure, confessing that God in his wrath has "taken me up and thrown me aside" (v. 10 NIV). Ashes and tears—the symbols of mourning—become his regular diet.

But see here a core dimension of supplication. The psalmist's trembling prayers turn to strong reassurance as he lifts his eyes from his wasted condition to the Lord of Zion. In his distress there is a solid confidence that the eternal God, who has been worshiped throughout all generations, will show favor to his people by one day returning from Zion. The distress that he presently knows is not the last word, neither for himself nor for his nation. Heaven and earth may perish like a worn-out garment (v. 26), but the eternal God will remain the same, and God's faithfulness will never end. God's servants will live in God's presence forever.

There is a wonderful line in Psalm 119 that captures the dynamic of supplication: "My eyes stay open through the watches of the night" (v. 148 NIV). It is suggestive of the plaintive cry that sometimes can't be expressed in words. So often our brooding and longing for God and for God's will to be done cannot find expression in words. That may be when we're doing our most effective supplication. In times like that, "the Spirit helps us in our weakness; for we do not know how to pray as we ought, but the very Spirit intercedes with sighs too deep for words. And God, who searches the heart, knows what is the mind of the Spirit, because the Spirit intercedes for the saints according to the will of God" (Romans 8:26-27).

Supplication, which includes petition and intercession, is a ministry of prayer that all of us should practice to some degree, and to which some may be called in a special way. The good news of the Bible is that God has established this universe in such a way that we humans are given the responsibility and opportunity of sharing in God's work. In God's economy, prayer is the powerful medium of exchange. We don't have to understand it to practice it. We simply have to accept the promises of God and believe that in the eternal scheme of things certain conditions are to be met by us in order that the Lord may act redemptively in our personal lives and in the world. The classic scriptural statement from the Old Testament is: "If my people who are called by my name humble themselves, pray, seek my face, and turn from their wicked ways [that's the *condition*], then I will hear from heaven, and will forgive their sin and heal their land [that's the *promise*]" (2 Chronicles 7:14).

The classic example from the New Testament is: "If you abide in me, and my words abide in you [that's the *condition*], ask for whatever you wish, and it will be done for you [that's the *promise*]" (John 15:7).

Prayer is God's idea.

Prayer is God's idea. We pray because God commands us to pray. In that light, there is a sense in which we ought not to ask for reasons for praying. Praying is like breathing. If we don't breathe, we don't live. If we don't pray, we don't live spiritually. In fact, if we don't pray, we die spiritually. Prayer is the premier source of our spiritual vitality.

This does not mean there are not questions—looming questions, tough questions—surrounding prayer, especially intercession. Prayer is all about God's sovereignty and God's will. What does our praying have to do with God's sovereign will? Is there any sense in which our praying changes God's will? What about a person's freedom? Much of our prayer, when we examine it, especially when we're interceding on behalf of others, has a strong focus on changing the direction, the attitude, or the action of another. What difference does our praying make in affecting the freedom of another?

What about healing? This is a plaguing question. When we've lived a long time and practiced prayer for a long time, it's obvious that sometimes when we pray for a person to be healed, that person is healed; but sometimes healing does not come. What dynamic does prayer have in the healing process? I don't know anyone who is clear about this; the mystery prevails. What we know is that when we pray, things happen that do not occur when we don't pray.

So, there are a lot of questions surrounding prayer. Without being irreverent, we contend that we don't have to answer those questions in order to pray. Why? Prayer is God's idea. God commands us to pray. It is clear that if we're to participate in God's economy, we are to pray.

So we make our petitions and intercessions, confident that God heals, forgives, leads, restores, comforts, prevents, corrects, challenges, inspires, judges, strengthens, and sustains. And, in a mysterious way that we may never understand, our praying is a channel by which God's ministry is affected in the lives of others and in situations. One requirement for effective supplication is our own willingness to be the answer to the prayers we pray.

Again, it is important that we be specific in our petitions and intercessions. It should go without saying that all of our praying is in the name of Christ and that our deepest desire is to focus our prayers in the will of God. We should, however, guard against adding "if it be your will" as a cover-up for our lack of faith or as an easy way out of personal involvement or costly demand.

If we keep vigilant in searching the Scripture, stay sensitive to God's presence through praise and worship, then we can be confident in our petitions and intercession. If we have confessed and have accepted forgiveness, if we have earnestly turned from our wicked ways and sought God's face, if we abide in the Lord, we can come boldly to the throne of grace presenting our personal longings and dreams, as well as petitions and intercessions for others and the world.

One of the neglected aspects of supplication is our intercession for the world, for the poor and oppressed of the world, for the plight of persons in spiritual darkness, for institutions and governmental systems that perpetuate injustice, and for the barriers that separate the human family and ravage relationships. Somehow, as Christians, we must cultivate a compassion that is so deep and so informed and empowered by the Spirit of Christ that we will not only know about the pain and suffering of others, but also enter that pain, feel it, and share it as far as possible. We are not called simply to know that others suffer or to assess the painful situations in which they may be. We are to feel the others' feelings—and not only feel, but also act when possible on behalf of the other.

"Devote yourselves to prayer, being watchful and thankful" (Colossians 4:2 NIV).

Pastoral Prayers for the Christian Year

From praying the hours to passion plays, Christians have creatively embodied the story of God throughout the history of the church. Thousands of years before, the Hebrew people were commemorating covenants and feasting at annual festivals, imaginatively rehearsing God's story, finding their voices, and playing their parts as their own chapters unfolded. Christians in the early epic of the church drew on centuries of practice as they boldly mapped out patterns of worship and prayer in order to stay faithfully narrated into the ever-unfolding drama of the New Creation. The Christian year, one of their early experiments, survives to the present day. Though dead and dormant in many present-day expressions, it is laden with generative power. The Christian year tracks the story of Scripture faithfully through the use of the Revised Common Lectionary, unfolding a drama into which we are continually invited to play a part.

The following pages unfurl the banners of Christ, defining pathways of prayer leading us ever deeper into the thickening plot of salvation. The prayers narrate the Christian year and, in doing so, pray the story. Scripture texts from the Revised Common Lectionary, particularly the psalms, provide the primary structure and influence of the prayers. We have drawn heavily from Year B of the cycle. We need to remember in our work of designing worship that the lections are not a rigid rule, but rather function like the colors on an artist's palate. We begin with Advent and then travel through Epiphany, to Lent and the Sundays of the Easter season, then to Pentecost, and finally to Ordinary Time.

Advent gifts us with an unlikely opportunity for new beginnings in the middle of the story. It is a crossroads of sorts; the intersection of first and second comings. A masterful plot device, Advent renarrates a distracted and dulled people into the storyline of Father, Son, and Holy Spirit. Advent opens new portals into the activity of the Trinity in the world and dynamic possibilities for purposeful participation. Fresh starts invite openness to the limitless capacities of the will of God, and yet they require waiting. Above all, Advent is a season of waiting. The Psalms teach us the practice of waiting at the intersection of attention and anticipation.

The Psalms teach us the practice of waiting at the intersection of attention and anticipation.

Coaching Your Congregation

In introducing the season of Advent, consider inviting your congregation to an experiment in praying with intentional posture. As a sign of patient openness, invite the congregation to stretch out the palms of their hands, placing them face up in their laps. Each week invite them to move their opened palms a bit higher (to the level of abdomen, heart, and then face). These same opened hands will be prepared to receive the Lord's Supper on Christmas Eve and perhaps to be lifted high with the candlelight of exaltation at the announcement of his birth. Sustaining this practice will engender a longer attention span in prayer while progressively raising the level of anticipation for the in-breaking Light of the World, the coming Lord Jesus.

First Sunday of Advent

Directions: As a sign of patient openness in a season of unimaginable gifts, invite the congregation to stretch out the palms of their hands, placing them face up in their laps during the prayer.

Give ear, O Shepherd of Israel, you who lead your people like a flock. "You who sit enthroned between the cherubim, shine forth"

(Psalm 80:1 NIV). From ages past no one has heard, no ear has perceived, no eye has seen any God besides you, who acts on behalf of those who wait for him (Isaiah 64:4 NIV).

Come, Holy Spirit, and inaugurate Advent in our midst. Come and open up the book of a new year of our Lord. Lift our hearts to long for your coming, and loose our longing to imagine your Kingdom.

We confess, Advent, the season of holy anticipation, has become for us a sign of anxiety. Like Martha, we busy ourselves with so many things, preparing for a celebration of our own design. We confess, our attention has become distraction. Our hearts, minds, and souls are divided as we literally surf the channels of our consumerist culture. Yet, O Lord, you are our Father; we are the clay, and you are our potter; we are all the work of your hand (Isaiah 64:8). Begin anew this Advent to shape us. Make us like Mary to sit at the feet of our Lord Jesus and discover the only necessary thing: your presence. Restore us, O God; let your face shine, that we may be saved. Shape these days of Advent into a season of undivided attention, of holy anticipation.

As we sing of peace on Earth and goodwill to all people, open our ears to hear the mournful songs of a war-torn world; the unquenchable cries of ordinary families such as our own whose losses are beyond our ability to comprehend. As we prepare to wrap the countless gifts our children will open on Christmas morning, open our hearts to the countless children for whom Christmas morning will be yet another day to survive. Lead us to respond to you in remembering those who will otherwise receive nothing; who are orphaned; whose parents are dead, distant, or imprisoned. Open our eyes to see those neighbors nearest to us who are lonely, afraid, sick, and suffering. We confess, our lifestyles have become enclaves of escape from the pain and suffering that surrounds us. Yet, O Lord, you are our Father; we are the clay, and you are our potter; we are all the work of your hand (Isaiah 64:8). Let this year be different, Lord. Shape our attention in these days of Advent into a lifestyle of love for neighbor and the needy.

Give ear, O Shepherd of Israel, you who lead your people like a flock. You who are enthroned on the cherubim, shine forth (Psalm 80:1). O that you would tear open the heavens and come down, so that the mountains would quake at your presence (Isaiah 64:1). As we remember and celebrate the birth of the baby in Bethlehem, let us not forget that the King is returning. We confess we have made ourselves at home in a world that is not our home. We know a time is coming when the sun will be darkened and the moon will not give its light; when the stars will be falling from heaven, and the powers in the heavens will be shaken. We know the Son of Man will come on the clouds with great power and glory and he will send out his angels to gather his elect from the ends of the earth to the ends of heaven (Mark 13:24-27). Stir in our hearts a holy anticipation for the world to come, and an undying urgency for the world that is passing away. By your Spirit make us watchful and wakeful. For you, O Lord, are our Father; we are the clay, and you are our potter; we are all the work of your hand (Isaiah 64:8).

> *Stir in our hearts a holy anticipation for the world to come,*
> *and an undying urgency for the world that is passing away.*

Come, Holy Spirit, and inaugurate Advent in our midst. Come and open up the book of a new year of our Lord. Hear us as we pray: Our Father, who art in heaven . . .

Second Sunday of Advent

Directions: As the season of patient waiting for God's gifts continues, invite the congregation to stretch out the palms of their hands, placing them a bit higher than last week—at the level of their abdomen.

Bold print signifies congregational response. Prior to praying, rehearse the litany with the congregation. Whenever the leader says, "And so we pray: prepare the way of the Lord." Invite the people to respond each time saying, **"Make his paths straight."** Practice this a few times prior to praying to enable the congregation to participate with confidence.

Almighty God, Father of our Lord, Jesus Christ, giver of the Holy Spirit, we gather to adore you in worship. Our heart's desire is to behold your glory. And yet if we are honest, we must admit that your glory is a sight we cannot even imagine and a reality for which we are scarcely prepared.

We hear reverberating in our souls the voice of one crying in the wilderness: Prepare the way of the Lord, make straight in the desert a highway for our God (Isaiah 40:3).

We want these days of Advent to be all celebration when they call us to a season of preparation. We want to rejoice, and John calls us to repent. We want to feast, and John calls us to fast. We want to be awash in the spirit of Christmas, and yet you speak of One who is coming who will baptize us with the Holy Spirit (Mark 1:1-8). For all our apparent strength, we confess with the prophet: our lives are as grass and our constancy like the flower of the field. The grass withers, the flower fades, but the word of our God will stand forever (Isaiah 40:6-7). Prepare us to behold the Christ, who is the glory of Christmas, the very Word of God made flesh. Surely his salvation is at hand for those who fear him, that his glory may dwell in our land (Psalm 85:9). And so we pray, prepare the way of the Lord: **Make his paths straight.**

Prepare us to behold the Christ, who is the glory of Christmas, the very Word of God made flesh.

Make us to know your ways, O Lord; teach us your paths. Lead us in your truth and teach us, for you are the God of our salvation; for you we wait all day long (Psalm 25:4-5). For with you one day is like a thousand years, and a thousand years are like one day (2 Peter 3:8). We know your return will not resemble your birth. On that day the heavens will pass away and the elements will be dissolved with fire and the earth and everything that is done on it will be disclosed (2 Peter 3:10). For the prepared, your glory will break forth with resplendent joy. For the unprepared, the same glory will be unmitigated terror. And so we pray, prepare the way of the Lord: **Make his paths straight.**

Bring down the high ways of our pride and arrogance. Lift up the cancerous valleys of sickness and depression and despair. Make smooth and straight the rough and crooked ways of our secret addictions to sin, our duplicitous ways of relationship, and our idolatrous love of money. Teach us the ways of humility, holiness, and godliness in our personal lives with our families, at work, and at play. Grant us courage to have the same integrity in every circumstance, to be the same person in every crowd. Teach us the ways of confession and

repentance that Christmas might become more than we ever imag-
ined. Prepare the way of the Lord: **Make his paths straight.**

We wait with longing for the day when faithfulness will spring up
from the ground and righteousness will look down from the sky. We
long for our lives and our church to be havens where steadfast love
and faithfulness meet, where righteousness and peace kiss each other
(Psalm 85:10-11). And as we wait, we pray, prepare the way of the
Lord: **Make his paths straight.** Together we pray the prayer of our
Lord, Our Father who art in heaven ...

PRAYING WITH POSTURE

expresses prayer ...

Conveying openness to the imaginative possibilities of
   God's intervention.

Open Hands signify an open heart

   • a willingness to release control

   • the propensity to give

   • an openness to freely receive

I

stretch

out my hands

to you;

my soul thirsts for you

like a parched land.

Psalm 143:6

44

Third Sunday of Advent

Directions: As the season of patient waiting for God's gifts continues, invite the congregation to stretch out the palms of their hands, placing them a bit higher than last week—at the level of their chest or heart.

Bold print signifies congregational response. Prior to praying, rehearse the litany with the congregation. Whenever the leader says, "We affirm that the Spirit of the Lord God is upon us," invite the people to respond each time, saying, **"Because the Lord has anointed us."** Practice this a few times prior to praying to enable the congregation to participate with confidence.

Almighty God, Father of our Lord, Jesus Christ, giver of the Holy Spirit, we gather to thank you for the gift of Christmas and for Advent, the season of preparation. With every week the lights grow brighter, our anticipation heightens, and our attention sharpens. We affirm that the Spirit of the Lord God is upon us: **because the Lord has anointed us** (Isaiah 61:1).

We are looking to you, the Mighty One, who has done great things. Teach us to worship you. Show us what it means for our souls to magnify the Lord. Instruct our spirits in what it means to rejoice in God our Savior (Luke 1:47-49). For you have done great things for us and we are filled with joy (Psalm 126:3). You have clothed us with the garments of salvation and covered us with the robes of righteousness (Isaiah 61:10).

We affirm that the Spirit of the Lord God is upon us: **because the Lord has anointed us.**

As the Son of God was formed in Mary's womb, so we bless you because your Spirit is forming his life within us for the sake of the world. In a time of unparalleled prosperity, we come before you to pray for the poor. Across the world, countless millions of children roam the streets in search of their next meal. We stand in your presence now on their behalf. In our own community, we witness some of the worst poverty of all: loneliness. Make us be good news to those who are poor. We take our stand with them now.

We affirm that the Spirit of the Lord God is upon us: **because the Lord has anointed us.**

We remember the brokenhearted, those whose loved ones have been lost to the hatred of war, the violence of disease, the injustice of death. As those among us stand, receive it as prayer and bind up their brokenness with our love.

We affirm that the Spirit of the Lord God is upon us: **because the Lord has anointed us.**

As your anointed, we plead for release to the captives. For many of our brothers and sisters around the world, the gospel means persecution and captivity. By your Spirit, cause some among us to stand now as prayer for their release and reward. We pray for friends and loved ones in our midst who have become prisoners in webs of addiction. Make our standing on their behalf become the seeds of your deliverance, the planting of the Lord, to display your glory (Isaiah 61:3).

Make our standing on their behalf become the seeds of your deliverance, the planting of the Lord, to display your glory.

We affirm that the Spirit of the Lord God is upon us: **because the Lord has anointed us.**

Give these for whom we pray a garland instead of ashes, the oil of gladness instead of mourning, the mantle of praise instead of a faint spirit (Isaiah 61:3). Fill their mouths with laughter and their tongues with shouts of joy so that it may be said among the nations, "The LORD has done great things for them" (Psalm 126:2).

Lord Jesus Christ, make our personal lives and our shared life together magnify you alone. Cause our glad tidings and good singing to combust into worship that moves the world. We bless you, the one who is, who was, and who is to come as we pray the prayer you taught us: Our Father who art in heaven ...

Fourth Sunday of Advent

Directions: As the season of patient waiting nears its apex, invite the congregation to stretch out the palms of their hands, placing them a bit higher than last week—at the level of their face or even extended above their heads as though reaching upward to greet and receive heaven's gift of the Son of God.

Invite the congregation to repeat Mary's prayerful declaration from Luke 1:38 as you begin to pray:

**Here am I, [echo]
the servant of the Lord; [echo]
let it be with me [echo]
according to your word. [echo]**

We will sing of your steadfast love, O LORD, forever; with our mouth we will proclaim your faithfulness to all generations. Blessed are you, O Lord, Emmanuel, the God who is with us. In the Garden you were with us as your Word shaped all of Creation. Through Abraham, Isaac and Jacob, you were with us as your Word crafted a covenant. You were with us in Egypt; your Word empowering our Exodus. You were with us at Sinai; your Word thundering in command. You were with us in the wilderness; your Word as daily bread. We declare that your steadfast love is established forever; your faithfulness is as firm as the heavens (Psalm 89:1-2).

You were with us at Christmas. Your Word stilled a star and conducted a choir of angels. Indeed, your Word became the very flesh of our flesh and bone of our bone. Your Word delivered unto us a Son who would save us from our sins.

Emmanuel, we bow down toward your holy temple and give thanks to your name for your steadfast love and your faithfulness; for you have exalted your name and your word above everything (Psalm 138:2).

Come, Holy Spirit, you who overshadowed the temple and the Virgin Mary with your glory. We humbly ask you to overshadow us such that when others encounter us they sense being with you. Transform our meager hospitality into heaven's welcome. Make us kind and good and gentle in ways that point to your presence in our midst. As others are with us, may they sense a growing measure of being with you.

Come, Holy Spirit. Overshadow. Hear our prayers for nothing is impossible for you.

[Insert specific concerns here.]

Come, Holy Spirit. Overshadow. Awaken our church to the glory of your nearness, the grandeur of your Word, and the joy of your mission in the world. In all things, grant us the grace of obedience. Hear our prayer with Mary, who said:

47

[Repeat after me]
> **Here am I,**
> **the servant of the Lord;**
> **let it be with me**
> **according to your word.**

And hear us as we pray the prayer Jesus taught us, saying: Our Father ...

Christmas Day

This prayer imagines an exuberant congregational response. The leader should instruct the congregation of their part, **"Christ is born today!"** to be spoken each time the leader's hands are lifted. And as the leader lifts his or her hands, he or she instructs the people to thrust their hands into the air as an act of worship as they declare Christ's birth. Practice a few times prior to the prayer.

Christmas prayer: Psalm 96; Isaiah 9:2-7; Luke 2:1-14; Titus 2:11-14

LEADER: Sing to the Lord a new song; sing to the Lord, all the earth (Psalm 96:1).

PEOPLE: **Christ is born today!**

LEADER: The people walking in darkness have seen a great light (Isaiah 9:2).

PEOPLE: **Christ is born today!**

LEADER: On those living in the land of the shadow of death a light has dawned (v. 2).

PEOPLE: **Christ is born today!**

LEADER: For as in the day of Midian's defeat, you have shattered the yoke that burdens them (v. 4).

PEOPLE: **Christ is born today!**

LEADER: Every warrior's boot used in battle and every garment rolled in blood will be destined for burning, will be fuel for the fire (v. 5).

PEOPLE: **Christ is born today!**

LEADER: The government will be on his shoulders. Of the increase of his government and peace there will be no end (vv. 6*b*, 7*a*).

PEOPLE: **Christ is born today!**

LEADER: He will reign on David's throne and over his kingdom, establishing and upholding it with justice and righteousness, from this time on and forever (v. 7*b*).

PEOPLE: **Christ is born today!**

LEADER: O Lord, Christ, your presence fills our hearts and our worship today. Splendor and majesty, strength and glory belong to you. We ascribe to you the glory due your name (Psalm 96:8). Wonderful Counselor, Mighty God, Everlasting Father, Prince of Peace (Isaiah 9:6).

> Christ, whose glory fills the skies,
>
> . . . .
>
> Sun of Righteousness, arise,
>
> . . . .
>
> Dayspring from on high be near;
> Daystar, in my heart appear.

We live with your Word. Today, the story that began not in a stable in Bethlehem, but in the garden of Creation; the story of your glory bestowed upon us, made in your image; the story of our fall, our grasping at control and power, wanting to be you (God), not like you; the story of patriarchs, priests, and prophets of exile and exodus; the story of deliverance and New Creation. We live with your Word and story and celebrate the Word, the Word that become flesh to dwell among us.

We think not only of Bethlehem, shepherds watching there, a frightened homeless woman having a baby, but also of Nazareth, the boy Jesus apprenticed to his carpenter father, a wandering prophet, teaching and preaching the eternal word that sounded strange even to those steeped in scriptures. How dumb our ears can be, how selective our hearing. We think of Calvary, its glory and dismay, especially of the now-announced Messiah, the Lamb of God, hanging on a tree.

We live with your Word today. We realize that the word of anybody is the attempt of a living being to communicate something. You are alive, O God, and your Word is not merely some expression of history or a repository of fact and truth or a collection to be handled gingerly, but something that is alive and even as sharp as a two-edged sword. We approach it not abstractly, but as emotionally involved as Mary and Joseph handling that new baby; as mystified

49

and challenged by it as they were as they sought to comprehend the meaning of shepherds and stars and wise men and angels.

We live with your Word, and it comes to focus in a special way today: God becomes incarnate, physical, in the world. God is made truly human in the womb of Mary and is born into the world just like us. Jesus Christ walks around, talks and eats with sinners, and doesn't always wash his hands. God reveals himself in human flesh—skin and teeth and tongue. He lives, he suffers, he dies. And Christ our Lord—announced and adored by sheep, shepherds, wise men, and angels; raised to glory the Father; and mighty to save, "for the grace of God has appeared, bringing salvation to all" (Titus 2:11 NRSV)—arose.

And so to you, O God, who sits upon the throne, and to Christ the Lamb be worship and praise, dominion and splendor forever and ever. Amen.

Epiphany is the sudden realization of something always known; or, to look at something all your life and one day finally see it. Epiphany unfolded as the kings arrived in Bethlehem to worship the Christ Child. More than a small town birthday party, this visitation heralded worldwide implications. The long and obscure journey of the wise men from distant nations revealed Jesus Christ as the Savior of all nations, the wisdom of God for the whole world.

Transform our meager hospitality into heaven's welcome.

Epiphany enlarges vision while focusing sight. The psalmist reveals the secret: watchfulness. As watchful eyes become fixed on Jesus Christ, the world comes clearly into focus. Our charitable ideals become transfigured by compassionate hope. Where before we saw insignificant solutions to overwhelming challenges, now we see the mustard seeds of faith becoming the very kingdom of God. In a secular season of new year's resolutions, the people of God must train their eyes to see into the vast implications of our God's resolve to save the whole world.

Epiphany of the Lord Sunday

Invite a posture of standing and looking up with eyes either open and fixed on a certain symbol or cross or window. Then, call the congregation to pray, repeating after the leader, line by line.

> To you [we] lift up our eyes,
>   O you who are enthroned in the heavens!
> As the eyes of servants
>   look to the hand of their master,
> as the eyes of a maid to the hand of her mistress,
> so our eyes look to the LORD our God,
>   until he has mercy upon us. (Psalm 123:1-2)

[A moment of pregnant silence]

"Praise the LORD! Praise the LORD, O my soul! I will praise the LORD as long as I live; I will sing praises to my God all my life long" (Psalm 146:1-2). We agree with the psalmist, "Happy are those whose help is the God of Jacob, whose hope is in the LORD their God, who made heaven and earth, the sea, and all that is in them; who keeps faith forever" (Psalm 146:5-6).

Faithful forever, you are the one hailed at birth by the kings of the earth as the very King of Kings. Though our nativity sets are already packed away in boxes, we remember today those wise ones whose starry pilgrimage declared the gospel; Jesus Christ would save the whole world. Father, we would trade all the presents of Christmas for the gift of Epiphany: the gift of seeing. Open the eyes of our hearts, Lord, and grant us the gift of Epiphany. We confess the extravagant gift of Christmas quickly becomes familiar. We tuck it away as a memory in the attic when you would have it become our light-filled life. We declare, O Lord, that because of your power, last year's Christmas will not become this year's yard sale.

We bless you because you execute justice for the oppressed and you give food to the hungry. You set prisoners free and open the eyes of the blind. You lift up those who are bowed down and you love the righteous. The Lord watches over the strangers; he upholds the orphan and the widow, but the way of the wicked he brings to ruin (Psalm 146:7-9).

Open the eyes of our hearts Lord and grant us the gift of epiphany: eyes that see. There are so many we pray for weekly whom we cease really to see. Grant us the grace to look long and deeply within to see them. Help us resist the temptation to define them by their need and instead to know them by your presence at work within. We lift their names before you now:

[List names and needs here.]

All your works shall give thanks to you, O LORD, and all your faithful shall bless you. They shall speak of the glory of your kingdom, and tell of your power, to make known to all people your mighty deeds, and the glorious splendor of your kingdom. Your kingdom is an everlasting kingdom, and your dominion endures throughout all generations. You, Lord are faithful in all your words, and gracious in all your deeds (Psalm 145:10-13).

Hear us as we pray our family prayer, the one Jesus taught us, saying: Our Father . . .

PRAYING WITH POSTURE

corroborates prayer . . .

Validating the signature of need and witnessing the sincerity of the plea.

Raised hands point to

- demonstrative, earnest faith

- a posture declaring devoted surrender

- willingness of spirit.

Hear my cry for mercy as I call to you for help,
as I lift up my hands
toward your Most Holy Place.

Psalm 28:2 NIV

52

Second Sunday of Epiphany

Directions: The season of Epiphany provides a good opportunity to express the hospitality of God's kingdom through praying for those persons who are not in relationship with Jesus Christ through their churches. Invite the congregation to become attentive to these persons, perhaps writing down their names, so they may more deeply carry these friends in their hearts. In the prayer below, opportunity is provided to whisper these names before God.

Almighty God our Father, Lord Jesus Christ, Holy Spirit, Wind of Heaven, we bless you joining the chorus of heaven, saying Holy, Holy, Holy is the Lord God Almighty, who was and is and is to come.

We remember in the beginning you created the heavens and the earth. The heavens opened, your Spirit descended, and your voice thundered, declaring creation's days and your glad pleasure. We declare with the psalmist, "The voice of the LORD is over the waters; the God of glory thunders, the LORD, over mighty waters" (Psalm 29:3).

Indeed "the earth is the LORD's and all that is in it, the world, and those who live in it; for he has founded it on the seas, and established it on the rivers" (Psalm 24:1-2).

Today we celebrate the awesome scene at the Jordan River when you, the Lord of heaven and earth, were baptized. The heavens opened; the Spirit, like a dove, descended; and your voice thundered, declaring the days of the New Creation and your glad pleasure. Indeed, "the voice of the LORD is over the waters; the God of glory thunders, the LORD, over mighty waters" (Psalm 29:3). We join the echo of the Father's voice in saying, you, Lord Jesus, are the Son of God. With you we are well pleased.

You are the Lord, our Good Shepherd. You make us lie down in green pastures; you lead us beside still waters; you restore our souls. You lead us in right paths for your name's sake (Psalm 23:1-3). We bless you for you have sent your Holy Spirit to breathe and brood over the darkness and chaos in our lives and our land.

Hear our concerns both near and far as we lift them to you:

[Insert specific petitions here.]

And hear the deep prayers of our hearts for those we love who seem not to know or walk with Christ. (I invite you now quietly to whisper those names before our Father.)

As we enter into the new year, we hoist our lives like a sail, saying Come Holy Spirit, rushing Wind of God, and blow us into the New Creation. We pray with the psalmist that you would:

> Teach us to number our days aright, that we may gain a heart of wisdom. (Psalm 90:12 NIV)

> Show us your ways, O LORD, teach us your paths ... and establish the work of our hands. (Psalm 25:4, 90:17 NIV)

> Grant us an undivided heart that we may worthily magnify your name. (Psalm 86:11, paraphrase)

With all of our hearts we want more of you, Lord. So come, Holy Spirit, and intensify the life of Jesus Christ in us that our lives might be lived for the sake of others.

We pray our family prayer, the one Jesus taught us, saying: Our Father ...

The Forty Days in Lent

In *Dora the Explorer,* the popular children's cartoon, Dora and her traveling companion, Boots the monkey, journey together on a weekly adventure, navigating from one destination to another. Map (the map) is their most treasured traveling companion. With Map's constant help, their journey dances gracefully back and forth between the expansive view of the forest and the hopeful yet insecure feelings they have walking among the trees. With liturgical gusto, the map dances and sings, "If there's a place you want to go I'm the one you need to know. I'm the map."

The best maps first disorient, challenging our false sense of reality with a truer representation of the real world. The central and perhaps most disorienting features of the year mapped by the Christian calendar are the forty days of Lent. The aim of the wilderness season is to orient through disorientation. We must become disoriented with the neatly packaged consumerist maps of our own design. Prayer can no longer be a laundry list of demands whose satisfaction determines our faith. Instead, prayer must become a circuit of pilgrimage sites, navigating us into the heart of God. We are attempting a map whose main topographical features are the birth, life, words, deeds, passion, death, ascension, resurrection, and return of Jesus Christ. Orientation in the world represented by this map consists in becoming lost to the neatly calendared boxes of our old one. "Whoever wants to save his life will lose it, but whoever loses his life for me will save it" (Mark 8:35 NIV). Translation: I am the map.

The map beckons, "Move beyond the Shire of predictable religion, and chance the perilous joy of a real encounter with the Holy God. Stop hiding, and risk disorientation with the cozy confines of our false self. Let fasting and weeping, confession and repentance lead us out of the shadows of secret sin and suffocating shame." The most abject sadness will be reserved for those who pursue a life of ministry while hiding from God. The most surprising grace awaits the pure in heart.

The most surprising grace awaits the pure in heart.

The poet T. S. Eliot may have said it best: "We must not cease from exploration and the end of all our exploring will be to arrive where we began and to know the place for the first time" ("Little Gidding V" [Four Quartets], *The Complete Poems and Plays of T. S. Eliot* [London: Faber & Faber, 1969]).

PRAYING WITH POSTURE

clarifies prayer ...

Creating space for confession; defining a relationship of intimate encounter.

Kneeling for prayer signals

- awe and reverence for a holy God

- a broken spirit and a contrite heart

- deep dependence on the mercy of God

O come, let us worship and bow down,

let us kneel before the Lord, our Maker!

For he is our God, and we are the people of his pasture,

and the sheep of his hand.

O that today you would listen to his voice!

Psalm 95:6-7

First Sunday in Lent

Print the litany below in the bulletin or on the screen as an introduction to the pastoral prayer (Psalm 95:6-9).

PEOPLE: O come let us worship and bow down, let us kneel before the LORD, our Maker! For he is our God, and we

are the people of his pasture, and the sheep of his hand. O that today you would listen to his voice!

LEADER: Do not harden your hearts, as at Meribah, as on the day at Massah in the wilderness, when your ancestors tested me, and put me to the proof, though they had seen my work.

Directions: Invite as many persons as wish to come to the chancel/altar area and kneel for this time of prayer. Others are invited to find a posture of humility in their seat. Kneeling or bowing would be appropriate. Give a period of complete silence once people are postured.

Almighty God, Father of our Lord Jesus Christ, promised Holy Spirit, we kneel before you in humble reverence and with grateful adoration. You are the only true God. There is no other (Isaiah 45:5-6). We are the people of your pasture and the sheep of your hand (Psalm 95:6).

We enter the forty days of Lent, the season of wilderness, with fear and trembling. The curse of our race echoes all about us and deep within our bones: from dust you have come and to dust you shall return (Genesis 3:19b). And yet we enter the desert gladly because you, our Good Shepherd, go before us. "And all of us, with unveiled faces, seeing the glory of the Lord as though reflected in a mirror, are being transformed into the same image from one degree of glory to another; for this comes from the Lord, the Spirit" (2 Corinthians 3:18). Come, Holy Spirit, bring your loving furnace of transformation in these days of wilderness, and make us a people who live for the glory of God and for the sake of others.

With one voice we declare that only you can lead us away from temptation. Only you can deliver us from evil. Our confession rests in the illumination of your Word. Our repentance depends on the wind of your Spirit.

Unto you O Lord, we lift up our souls. O God, in you we trust; do not let us be put to shame; do not let our enemies exult over us. Do not let those who wait for you be put to shame (Psalm 25:1-3a). Make us to know your ways, O Lord; teach us your paths. Lead us in your truth and teach us, for you are the God of our salvation; for you we wait all day long (vv. 4-5). Do not remember the sins of our youth or our transgressions; according to your steadfast love remember us, for your goodness' sake, O Lord! Good and upright is the Lord; therefore he instructs sinners in the way. You lead the humble in what is right, and teach the humble your way. All of your paths are steadfast love and faithfulness for those who keep your covenant and your decrees (vv. 7-10).

We would be a covenant people who reflect and refract your love for the world. Make us ever mindful of the needs of others, Lord.

[Insert local and global petitions here.]

Our eyes are ever toward you, Lord, for you will pluck our feet out of the net. Turn to us and be gracious to us, for we are lonely and afflicted. Relieve the troubles of our hearts, and bring us out of our distress. Consider our afflictions and our troubles and forgive all our sins (Psalm 25:15-18). May integrity and uprightness preserve us, for we wait for you (v. 21).

Hear our family prayer as we pray together the way Jesus taught us: Our Father ...

Second Sunday in Lent

Print the litany below in the bulletin or on the screen as an introduction to the pastoral prayer (Psalm 95:6-9).

PEOPLE: **O come, let us worship and bow down, let us kneel before the Lord, our Maker! For he is our God, and we are the people of his pasture, and the sheep of his hand. O that today you would listen to his voice!**

LEADER: Do not harden your hearts, as at Meribah, as on the day at Massah in the wilderness, when your ancestors tested me, and put me to the proof, though they had seen my work.

Directions: Invite as many persons as wish to come to the chancel/altar area and kneel for this time of prayer. Others are invited to find a posture of humility in their seat. Kneeling or bowing would be appropriate. Give a period of complete silence once people are postured.

Almighty God, Father of our Lord Jesus Christ, promised Holy Spirit, we kneel before you in humble reverence and with grateful adoration. You are the only true God. There is no other. We are the people of your pasture, and the sheep of your hand (Psalm 95:6).

We bless you for calling us to a season of confession and repentance. Though we are a people of unparalleled promise, we so readily wander away from you, precious Lord Jesus. We hear you calling us, to deny ourselves and take up our cross and follow you. We are eager to join you on the mountaintop where life is gloriously transfigured, and yet with Peter, we readily rebuke you for leading us to the cross.

O Lord, you have searched us and known us. You know when we sit down and when we rise up; you discern our thoughts from far away. You search out our path and our lying down and are acquainted with all our ways. Even before a word is on our tongue, O Lord, you know it completely. You hem us in, behind and before, and lay your hand upon us (Psalm 139:1-5). Where can we go from your spirit? Or where can we flee from your presence (v. 7)?

Come, Holy Spirit, and turn your search lights in our souls. Search us and know our hearts; test us and know our thoughts. See if there is any wicked ways in us, and lead us in the way everlasting (Psalm 139:23-24). Grant us the grace of self-knowledge and confession that we might renounce and forsake the duplicitous lies of our lives. *[Pause for silent prayer.]*

And as you search us out, save us from the snare of self-absorption. Let your work of transformation not become a project of perfecting ourselves. Keep us ever mindful of the needs of others, both near and far.

[Insert local and global petitions here.]

How weighty to us are your thoughts, O God! How vast is the sum of them! We try to count them—they are more than the sand; we come to the end—we are still with you (Psalm 139:17-18).

Hear our family prayer as we pray together the way Jesus taught us: Our Father ...

PRAYING WITH POSTURE

amplifies prayer ...

Magnifying the heart's intent beyond the ability of words.

Laying prostrate before the Lord points to

- the presence of Royalty or Deity

- a sense of being completely awe struck

- acute awareness of humility and unworthiness to stand

Third Sunday in Lent

Print the litany below in the bulletin or on the screen as an introduction to the pastoral prayer (Psalm 95:6-9).

PEOPLE: **O come let us worship and bow down, let us kneel before the LORD, our Maker! For he is our God, and we are the people of his pasture, and the sheep of his hand. O that today you would listen to his voice!**

LEADER: Do not harden your hearts, as at Meribah, as on the day at Massah in the wilderness, when your ancestors tested me, and put me to the proof, though they had seen my work.

Directions: Invite as many persons as wish to come to the chancel/altar area and kneel for this time of prayer. Others are invited to find a posture of humility in their seat. Kneeling or bowing would be appropriate. Give a period of complete silence once people are postured.

Spirit of Jesus, come. Bend us, O Lord. We want to make room for you today.

Out of the depths we cry to you, O Lord. Lord, hear our voice! Let your ears be attentive to the voice of my supplications! If you, O Lord, should mark iniquities, Lord, who could stand? But there is forgiveness with you, so that you may be revered (Psalm 130:1-4). You do not merely forgive us, but call us your children. You have named us heirs with Christ—brothers and sisters of Jesus! You have raised us up with Christ and seated us with him in the heavenly realms—and we are amazed!

How can you be so good to us? How dare you treat sinners so? How scandalous—the Word has become flesh, the Creator a creature, and taken our humanity into the eternal communion of the Trinity! Can we doubt that angels long to look into these things? O God, forgive us for taking it for granted!

Because, by your grace, you have made us partakers of the divine nature. You have deigned to inhabit us with your Holy Spirit, turning sinners into temples. Even as your glory filled the tabernacle in the wilderness, and the temple, so now have you filled us with your radiant essence. And you have invited us into the city of the living God, the heavenly Jerusalem; and we join the hosts of heaven, the angels and archangels, the cherubim and seraphim, and spirits of righteous ones made perfect; and we cry out with them, "Holy, holy, holy Lord, God of power and might. Heaven and earth are full of your glory. Hosanna in the highest. Blessed is he who comes in the name of the Lord. Hosanna in the highest."

By your grace you have made us partakers of the divine nature.

What kind of God are you? You exalt dust. You eat with sinners. And, though we have been proud and stiff-necked and deaf to your voice, you still speak to us. You still meet your people in the wilderness. And you say:

> I am *YHWH*, your Holy One, Israel's Creator and King, I am YHWH, who opened a way through the waters, making a dry path through the sea. I called forth the mighty army of Egypt with all its chariots and horses.

I drew them beneath the waves, and they drowned,
their lives snuffed out like a smoldering candlewick.
But forget all that—it is *nothing* compared to what
    I am going to do.
Behold, I will do something new,
Now it will spring forth;
Will you not be aware of it?
I will even make a roadway in the wilderness,
    Rivers in the desert.
The beasts of the field will glorify Me,
The jackals and the ostriches,
Because I have given waters in the wilderness
And rivers in the desert,
To give drink to My chosen people.
The people whom I formed for Myself
    will declare My praise.[1] (Isaiah 43:15-21 NLT and NASB)

So meet us, Lord, here where we are. We welcome your new work in our lives and in the world. Amen.

Fourth Sunday in Lent

Print the litany below in the bulletin or on the screen as an introduction to the pastoral prayer (Psalm 95:6-9).

PEOPLE: **O come, let us worship and bow down, let us kneel before the LORD, our Maker! For he is our God, and we are the people of his pasture, and the sheep of his hand. O that today you would listen to his voice!**

LEADER: Do not harden your hearts, as at Meribah, as on the day at Massah in the wilderness, when your ancestors tested me, and put me to the proof, though they had seen my work.

Directions: Invite as many persons as wish to come to the chancel/altar area and kneel for this time of prayer. Others are invited to find a posture of humility in their seat. Kneeling or bowing would be appropriate. Give a period of complete silence once people are postured.

O God, you are our God, we seek you, our souls thirst for you; our flesh faints for you, as in a dry and weary land where there is no water (Psalm 63:1). As a deer longs for flowing streams, so our souls long for you, O God. Our souls thirst for God, for the living God. When shall we come and behold the face of God? (Psalm 42:1-2).

We remember your people in the wilderness, and we confess to being like them. You forgive all our iniquity, heal all our diseases, redeem our lives from the Pit, crown us with steadfast love and mercy, and satisfy us with good as long as we live (Psalm 103:3-5). And yet we incessantly complain with our insatiable desires. We confess we have desired your blessings more than we have delighted in you.

And so, God, what we need is an encounter with you. What we need is to be changed and transformed—not just for a moment, not just for a few minutes before lunch, but completely renovated, overturned, flipped upside down and inside out. We need to be changed, not just as individuals, Father, but as a community, as a body, as your church.

Do a deep work in us this morning, God. Dig into the fibers of our hearts, slicing through our self-sufficiency and security. We are a stiff-necked people, O God, but you so deeply love us. Release your Spirit upon us, we pray, to convict us, to sanctify us, and to empower us to be Kingdom people. Could you really welcome your prodigal church with open arms? We are tired of religion—we want to be the friends of God! And we want to know you, Lord Christ, in your sufferings as well as in your resurrection. Let us not take your cross for granted. And even in our repentance, let us remember that your cross is bigger than our sin. Your cross has borne our shame. Your broken body has sealed our eternity. Your blood makes us clean. You who had no sin became sin for us. And in your grace we now stand, begging to be made more like you, longing to be changed by you, hoping to be counted as your good and faithful servants.[2]

Your cross has borne our shame. Your broken body has sealed our eternity. Your blood makes us clean. You who had no sin became sin for us.

Restore us as a people who find their lives in losing them for the sake of others. In your mercy, hear our prayers for those near and far:

[Insert petitions here.]

Because you are exalted, Triune God, over all the earth! You have defeated sin and death. You have triumphed over every principality and power and authority. And, oh mystery, you have conquered us, also, bending our proud necks beneath your holy feet. How can we but delight in you, O God? How can we help but sing your praises? Open our hearts, now to extol you—in the Name of the Father, Son, and Holy Spirit—and hear us as we pray the prayer of your heart, the one Jesus taught us, saying: Our Father ...

Fifth Sunday in Lent

Print the litany below in the bulletin or on the screen as an introduction to the pastoral prayer (Psalm 95:6-9).

PEOPLE: **O come, let us worship and bow down, let us kneel before the LORD, our Maker! For he is our God, and we are the people of his pasture, and the sheep of his hand. O that today you would listen to his voice!**

LEADER: Do not harden your hearts, as at Meribah, as on the day at Massah in the wilderness, when your ancestors tested me, and put me to the proof, though they had seen my work.

Directions: Invite as many persons as wish to come to the chancel/altar area and kneel for this time of prayer. Others are invited to find a posture of humility in their seat. Kneeling or bowing would be appropriate. Give a period of complete silence once people are postured.

Eternal God, our heavenly Father, we bless you for these wilderness days of Lent. We thank you for the way your Son, our great High Priest Jesus, teaches us that we live not by bread alone, but by every word that comes from your mouth. We thank you for the way the Holy Spirit, the flame of love, takes your Word and not only nourishes us, but also enflames it into a furnace of transformation.

We treasure your word in our hearts, so that we may not sin against you. Blessed are you, O Lord; teach us your statutes. With our lips we declare all the ordinances of your mouth. We delight in the way of your decrees as much as in all riches. We will meditate on your precepts and fix our eyes on your ways. We will delight in your statutes; we will not forget your word (Psalm 119:11-16).

You desire truth in the inward being; therefore teach me wisdom in my secret heart (Psalm 51:6). Father, let these days not pass before we have made a good confession to you, one representing authenticity and honesty. "Let us not be like the horse or the mule, which have no understanding but must be controlled by bit and bridle or they will not come to you" (Psalm 32:9 NIV). Instead, create in us clean hearts, O God, and put a new and right spirit within us. Do not cast us away from your presence, and do not take your Holy Spirit from us. Restore to us the joy of your salvation, and sustain in us a willing spirit (Psalm 51:10-12).

Restore to us the joy of your salvation, and sustain in us a willing spirit.

We thank you for the gift of a season to be honest with you, ourselves, and one another. Let our confession become like a hoisting of our lives—like a sail on the mast of the cross. May the wind of the Holy Spirit blow our lives into new courses, toward a life that truly matters.

Make us ever mindful of the needs of others both near and far.

[Insert global and local petitions here.]

As we journey nearer the cross in preparation for Easter, prepare the way for the Lord. We are eager for the New Covenant he has made with us to become renewed in our lives once again. We pray now, together, the prayer Jesus taught us, saying: Our Father ...

Palm Sunday

Mark 11:1-11   Psalm 118   John 12:12-16

Directions: In the prayer, invite the congregation to declare, **"Hosannah! Blessed is he who comes in the name of the Lord!"** when the leader says, "We join the company of heaven, declaring." Practice this a few times prior to the prayer, coaching an exuberant response from the people.

To you, Eternal Father, we lift our voices in praise and thanksgiving.

To you, O Lamb of God, who takes away the sins of the world (John 1:29), we sing as we begin this holy week. Hosannah! Blessed is he who comes in the name of the Lord (John 12:13).

Holy Spirit, sanctify our imagination that we might climb Calvary's mournful mountain and behold God's own sacrifice, "who, though he was in the form of God, did not regard equality with God as something to be exploited, but emptied himself, taking the form of a slave, being born in human likeness. And being found in human form, he humbled himself and became obedient to the point of death—even death on a cross" (Philippians 2:6-8 NRSV).

Holy Spirit, sanctify our imagination. We would see Jesus as he set his face steadfastly to go to Jerusalem (Luke 9:51). We join the company of heaven, declaring:

PEOPLE: **Hosannah! Blessed is he who comes in the name of the Lord!**

LEADER: We would see Jesus, entering the city on a humble donkey, a vivid symbol of the nature of his kingship. We join the company of heaven, declaring:

PEOPLE: **Hosannah! Blessed is he who comes in the name of the Lord!**

LEADER: We would see Jesus in the judgment hall, accused, reviled, arraigned, never saying a "mumblin'" word. We join the company of heaven, declaring:

PEOPLE: **Hosannah! Blessed is he who comes in the name of the Lord!**

LEADER: We would see Jesus, mercilessly beaten, bound, spit upon, scorned—previous cries of adoration turn now into screams of derision and condemnation, crucify him. We join the company of heaven, declaring:

PEOPLE: **Hosannah! Blessed is he who comes in the name of the Lord!**

LEADER: We would see Jesus, nailed to the tree, dying in anguish and bitter passion, his love unswerving, his grace conferred on a repentant criminal, the Lamb of God taking away the sins of the world. We join the company of heaven, declaring:

PEOPLE: **Hosannah! Blessed is he who comes in the name of the Lord!**

Holy Spirit, sanctify our imagination, that we might mark this miracle of time—God's own sacrifice—complete: "It is finished" (John 19:30). We would see Jesus, this beaten, broken, crucified man who indeed was God's Son, the living presence of God, whom we confess we don't know well enough. So teach us, Holy Spirit, this week. Teach us more about Jesus that we may know more about God—a God who is good and whose steadfast love endures forever (Psalm 118:1).

Make real to the world, through us your church, that the stone that the builders rejected is our chief cornerstone (Psalm 118:22). We will love and serve and suffer. We will walk the way of the cross for the sake of the world. And when we are asked why, as those who borrowed the donkey for Jesus to ride into Jerusalem, we will respond, "The Lord needs it" (Mark 11:3). The Lord needs our passionate witness; the Lord needs our compassionate acts of love; the Lord needs our demonstration of "Father, forgive them"; the Lord needs our flint-faced commitment to stay with him in serving the least of these, in staying awake and praying in redemptive intercession for his coming kingdom.

Deliver us, Lord, from our dullness to the message of this passion week; quicken us from our deadness that we may live and recount the deeds of the Lord (Psalm 118:17). May we enter your presence through gates of praise and give thanks to you forever (v. 19). Mercifully grant that we may walk the way of Jesus' suffering and also share in his resurrection through Jesus Christ our Lord, who lives and reigns with you and the Holy Spirit, one God, forever and ever. Amen.

He is risen indeed!

Easter ushers in a season of unparalleled prayer, a time when longing gives way to living; when repentance rises up into praise. Prayer must move from request for funds to extravagant spending; from asking God to write the check to obeying his command to cash it. He is risen indeed! Everything has changed. Our God is making all things new.

"Praise the LORD! Praise God in his sanctuary; praise him in his mighty firmament! Praise him for his mighty deeds; praise him according to his surpassing greatness!" (Psalm 150:1-2).

Easter calls not for a kneeling examination of conscious and ash-bent confession of sin, but for an upright awareness of lingering unbelief and heaven-bound confessions of faith. Easter opens eyes to behold his hands and side and to declare, "My Lord and my God!"

Get creative, church. Praise him with trumpet sound; praise him with lute and harp! Praise him with tambourine and dance; praise him with strings and pipe! Praise him with loud clanging cymbals!

"Let everything that breathes praise the LORD! Praise the LORD!" (Psalm 150:6).

PRAYING WITH POSTURE

elevates prayer ...

To the place of readiness, declaring a distilled determination to be involved in the answer.

Standing upright for prayer signifies

- the humble victory of our God

- a willingness to walk on into the answers

- bold intercession on behalf of the world.

I was glad when they said to me,
"Let us go to the house of the Lord!"
Our feet are standing
within your gates, O Jerusalem.

Psalm 122:1-2

Easter Sunday

Directions: Instruct the congregation to respond with, **"Your steadfast love endures forever,"** each time the leader says, **"Because we know."** Practice this exchange a few times prior to the prayer time.

Isaiah 25:6-9   Psalm 118   1 Corinthians 15:1-11   John 20:1-18

Lord of power and might, you are sovereign over life and death and we praise your holy name on this glorious day of resurrection. Far, far more than a happy ending to a sad story, this day is a victory celebration for your conquest of death and an awesome beginning for a new and eternal life.

In the beginning, before the marking of time, darkness was over the surface of the deep (Genesis 1:2). And you spoke your word, "Let there be light" (Genesis 1:3). Then in the fullness of time the Word that was in the beginning (John 1:1) became flesh and dwelt among us (John 1:14). In him was life and light so powerful that, in our sin, we sought to put it out. But your redemption plan prevailed because your steadfast love endures forever (Psalm 118:2). For our sake you gave your Son, Jesus, to death on the cross; and through his glorious resurrection, you delivered us from sin and death. With Paul, we affirm that by this gospel (1 Corinthians 15:2), this gospel of Jesus—his life, teaching, suffering, death, and resurrection—we are saved.

For many of us here today, our experience is that of Mary Magdalene: we come while it is still dark (John 20:1). A member of our family is not with us. We don't even know where he or she is.

The death of our loved one still hangs like a dark cloud over us, and we have not yet claimed the certainty of resurrection.

[Note: Invite the congregation to name specific experiences in the congregation, community, and world that represent darkness before the dawn, or the worship leader will add specific experiences.]

Evil forces are crucifying goodness and truth. It is Friday for peace and justice, which are still on the cross, waiting for an Easter triumph.

69

Some of us are here while it is still dark. We confess that the risen Christ may have already come to us, but we do not realize it was Jesus (1 Corinthians 15:14). We have heard the word of resurrection, and something deep inside us—who we are and who we want to be—has come running here today (John 20:3) to experience your presence and power.

We believe; help our unbelief that we may confidently claim that we will not die but will have life and proclaim what you have done (Psalm 118:17). We rehearse what we commit ourselves to as an ongoing witness; your steadfast love endures forever (v. 2).

You have destroyed the shroud that enfolds all people (Isaiah 25:7). Because we know:

PEOPLE: **Your steadfast love endures forever.**
LEADER: You will wipe away our tears (Isaiah 25:8) of loneliness and loss because we know
PEOPLE: **Your steadfast love endures forever.**
LEADER: You will forgive our sins and heal our land because we know
PEOPLE: **Your steadfast love endures forever.**
LEADER: Now it is so. You have swallowed up death forever ... because we know
PEOPLE: **Your steadfast love endures forever.**

May your steadfast love sustain us as we pass on the gospel we have received (1 Corinthians 15:3) through Jesus Christ our Lord, who lives and reigns with you in the unity of the Holy Spirit, now and forever, our risen Lord who taught us to pray: Our Father, who art in heaven ...

Second Sunday of Easter

Acts 4:32-35   Psalm 133   1 John 1:1–2:2   John 20:19-31

O God, who, by the glorious resurrection of your Son Jesus, destroyed death and fulfilled your promise of life forevermore (Psalm 133:3), grant that we may be raised with him to newness of life and abide in him (John 15:14) that peace may be ours.

Make real to us the price of peace. Emblazon on our minds the wounds in Jesus' hands and side that we may never forget that he is the atoning sacrifice for our sins and the sins of the whole world (1 John 2:2). Make our joy complete (1 John 1:4) as we confess our sin. This is not easy, Lord, to acknowledge that we are sinners. We have chosen our own way rather than yours. As individuals and as a church, we have not been obedient. Confront us now with our deception (1 John 1:8), our walking in darkness when we claim a saving relationship with you (1 John 1:6). In silence now, we name our most glaring sin, and we pray that you will reveal that which we have hidden for so long that only the blazing light of your presence will bring it to light.

[Note: *Allow at least one full minute of complete silence. In the next paragraph each time you see a // mark, please pause with a few seconds of deliberate silence before continuing.*]

Lord Jesus, we claim now our advocacy with the Father (1 John 2:1). //
Make the joy of our salvation a precious oil of healing and reconciliation, the blessing of the Lord for others (Psalm 133:2). //
Breathe on us your peace, Lord Jesus (John 20:21). As our Father, you breathed life at first creation (Genesis 2:7), breathe into us now, living Christ, your Holy Spirit (John 20:22), that we may be recreated as peace-bringers and joy-givers. //
Open our eyes that we may see the needs of others. //
Open our ears that we may hear their cries. //
Open our hearts that we may provide them comfort and hope. //
May no needy person among us be without the care and attention of your people who know how precious it is to live together in the unity of your peace (Acts 4:34, Psalm 133:1). //
Eternal God, open the eyes of our faith that we may behold all the redeeming work of your resurrected Son, our Savior and Lord, who lives and reigns with you in the unity of the Holy Spirit, one God, now and forever. Amen.

[Note: *We do not always close the prayers with the Lord's Prayer. Use your discretion according to the way you have designed the service as to whether to include it.*]

Third Sunday of Easter

Acts 3:12-19   Psalm 4   1 John 3:1-7   Luke 24:36b-48

God of Abraham, Isaac, and Jacob; God of our ancestors Sarah, Miriam, Mary, and Martha; God of the resurrection who glorified Jesus by raising him from the dead (Acts 3:13), we worship you and praise your name. We come rejoicing today because you answer when we call (Psalm 4:1, 3).

Enliven our imaginations today in order that we may see not a ghost, but the risen, living Jesus (Luke 24:37). We remember how Jesus showed the wounds in His hands and feet that His disciples would know this was the same Jesus with whom they had shared for three years, the same One who a few days before they had seen suffering and dying on an awful cross (vv. 39-40). This was not a ghost, not one who only seemed to be Jesus. He was Jesus, the carpenter from Nazareth, who had suffered death and, by God's power in the resurrection, had been transformed into a new mode of life. Enliven our imaginations that we may experience fully and speak boldly of this One who can empower us to see him as he is.

We know that we become like what or whom we worship of.

We know that we become like what or whom we worship. So, we worship you, Lord, Jesus, claiming the promise that when we see you, we will become like you (1 John 3:2).

We know, Father, that it is only your love through Jesus Christ that saves us, heals us, reconciles us, and makes us your children. Though we are sinners, you declare us innocent.

We know that possibility can be realized only through your Son, Jesus Christ, who is our Savior. There is salvation in no one else, no other name by which we might be saved (Acts 4:12). He who knew no sin became sin for us that we may be righteous in your sight (2 Corinthians 5:21). Knowing this, we confess. We have sinned and fallen short of your intention for us. In silence now, we name our particular sinful attitudes and actions that, without confession and repentance, will keep us separated from you.

[Note: Please allow for at least one full minute of silence before proceeding with the prayer.]

We confess our sin and failure as a congregation:

We have not seen the needs and heard the cries of the poor.

We have been seduced by and sought security in our material wealth.

We have been afraid to take a stand for righteousness because public opinion is against us.

Too often we confuse being a good American with being a faithful Christ-follower.

We are more committed to maintenance of our facilities than to ministry in the community.

We are unfaithful in our financial stewardship and excuse our lack of vision and faithfulness on our lack of money.

Lord Jesus, you are the Author of life, whom God raised from the dead (Acts 3:15) so that our sins may be wiped out and that times of refreshment may come (vv. 19-20). Thank you for making our salvation possible through your death and resurrection.

Eternal Father, may we live in repentance that the light of your face may shine upon us (Psalm 4:6). Give us the confidence today and all days to lie down in peace and sleep, for you alone, O Lord, will keep us safe (v. 8).

Hear us, Father, as we pray the prayer Jesus taught us: Our Father ...

Fourth Sunday of Easter

Directions: As an introduction to this time of prayer, the leader will say something along these lines: "No portion of Scripture is more familiar to the people of God than the Twenty-third Psalm. Seldom, however, do we repeat it together in corporate worship. As we come to this time of prayer, let us share this word of God together."

[Note: Either have the Twenty-third Psalm printed in the bulletin or on the screen, or invite persons to access a common translation if a pew Bible is available.]

Acts 4:5-12   Psalm 23   1 John 3:16-24   John 10:11-18

Eternal God, your dominion extends to the farthest planet, and your glory is not only beyond expression, but even beyond imagination. Yet you have chosen to enter our realm of life as the Good Shepherd who knows our names, the names of the most ignored and forgotten persons among us. You know even the fall of a sparrow. Shepherd God, we bless your name. We are here in this place at this time, so we come boldly into your presence, knowing that we are welcome.

You prepare a table before us and we thank you.

For the world you have created and for the gift of life to each of us, we thank you.

For giving yourself to us in Jesus Christ, whose holy life, suffering, death, and glorious resurrection have delivered us from slavery to sin and death, we thank you.

For the special table you have prepared, for the sacrament of holy communion, we thank you. You gather the sheep of your flock at this table to express your love and care, to remind us that there is one flock and one shepherd, to give us a foretaste of the heavenly banquet, to send us forth to be the bread for the world and the witness to love, and to serve and to gather other sheep who do not yet belong to our fold (John 10:16).

Send us forth to be the bread for the world, witnesses to love, and servants to serve.

Jesus, our Good Shepherd, though the world continues to reject your leadership in the paths of righteousness and peace (Psalm 23:3), we will walk with you. When the way is dark, be our light; when our feet grow weary, be our strength and restore our souls; when fear presses us to turn back, even to hide, call us by name that we will know you are there. If we have wandered from the fold, if we feel like a lost sheep, come now, Shepherd Lord, and rescue us.

In the jungle of life, we need a shepherd, not a hired hand, not a pretender. There are wolves aplenty that would scatter and destroy us (John 10:12). We need a shepherd who will lay down his life for us, lay it down and take it up again (John 10:17). No other shepherd than you, Jesus, does that (Acts 4:12).

In gratitude for your shepherding love, we will love one another (1 John 3:18). As you, Lord Jesus, have revealed the fullness of God by your love, may our love give at least a hint of God's presence to those around us. And as we follow you more closely, may your life in us grow until all those around us know that you abide in us (1 John 3:24).

O God, our Good Shepherd, whose son Jesus revealed your shepherding love, grant that when we hear his voice we may know him who calls us each by name and follow where he leads; he who, with you and the Holy Spirit, lives and reigns, one God, forever and ever. Amen.

Fifth Sunday of Easter

Acts 8:26-40   Psalm 22:25-31   1 John 4:7-21   John 15:1-8

All honor and praise are yours today, loving God, and we join your lovers and followers and those who are seeking you in worship to bow down, to remember, to turn to you (Psalm 22:27, 29). The heart of our praise is the celebration and renewal of our vows (v. 25) and the conviction that you are sovereign, that dominion belongs to you (v. 28), and that one day all will bow down (v. 29) and confess that your resurrected Son is Lord.

In our baptism, we confessed our faith in Jesus Christ as our Savior and Lord. Your word promises that if we make that confession, you abide in us and we abide in you (1 John 4:15). Inspire us, Father, to accept this awesome privilege of abiding. We rejoice in our relationship to Jesus. He is the vine; we are the branches (John 15:5). May we learn the lesson of abiding in him by studying and responding to your word *[pause]*, by spending time in prayer *[pause]*, by deliberate conversation with those who are seeking your way *[pause]*, through worship, and by all the means of grace your church provides *[pause]*.

May the Holy Spirit be for us the sap that flows from the vine into the branches to give us life. Apart from that energy, we will be barren and lifeless and bear no fruit for your Kingdom.

We shudder, vine-tending God, at the possibility of our lives being so purposeless, so unfocused, so lacking in passion, so separated from Jesus and void of kingdom fruit, that we would be cut off and thrown into a waste heap. Deliver us from life patterns of inattention to you *[pause]*, lack of love and concern for others *[pause]*, preoccupation with material security and success *[pause]*, destructive habits—anything, Lord, that would cut us off from the Spirit energy flowing from the vine.

Your Word is clear: suffering love, the cross, and the empty tomb have dealt with sin once and for all. We are cleansed by the Word (John 15:3). Your overflowing love welcomes all and empowers us to love as you love (John 15:10). Thank you, Father. May your love be perfected in us (1 John 4:12) that you may live in us and be seen in us by others.

> *Your overflowing love welcomes all and empowers us to love as you love.*

You call us to witness, and we know that our witness must be rooted in Scripture if we are to proclaim the good news of Jesus (Acts 8:35). All around us are people looking for guidance, needing and desiring someone to give them attention and to care about them.

[Note: Name here specific groups in the community such as single parents, children living in poverty, teachers in our public schools, and political leaders.]

The key that will unlock the heart of another and give power to our verbal witness is your love in us, overflowing in concrete expressions of practical concern. May we be the guarantee of your promise that future generations will be told about the Lord (Psalm 22:30) and deliverance proclaimed to peoples yet unborn (v. 31). So, in the days ahead, may each of us think of ourselves as an act of God, the breath of God's love for the sake of others, as we abide in Christ, who taught us to pray, Our Father . . .

Sixth Sunday of Easter

Directions: Print the litany below (ending with the lyrics to the hymn) in the bulletin or on the screen. Invite the congregation to affirm the response joyfully: **We sing a new song.** If possible, invite the congregation to sing the first verse of "O For a Thousand Tongues to Sing," without musical accompaniment. If not possible, recite the words in unison. If used in a setting in which the litany cannot be printed, the leader might simply instruct the congregation, "When I lift my hand, you respond: **We sing a new song.**"

Acts 10:44-48   Psalm 98   1 John 5:1-6   John 15:9-17

Eternal God, we are singing a new song during these Easter days because you have done marvelous things (Psalm 98:1). Even if we do not sing and make a joyful noise, the seas will continue to roar in praise, the floods clap their hands, and the hills sing together (vv. 7-8).

LEADER: In gratitude for your beautiful and bountiful creation,
PEOPLE: **we sing a new song.**
LEADER: In humble awe for your becoming one with us in our humanity,
PEOPLE: **we sing a new song.**
LEADER: In earnest desire to follow your teaching,
PEOPLE: **we sing a new song.**
LEADER: In joyful praise for your suffering, death, and resurrection,
PEOPLE: **we sing a new song.**
LEADER: In speechless praise, because you have claimed us not as servants, but as friends, we're silent—but still singing a new song.

[Be silent and still.]
Because you remembered your steadfast love and faithfulness and all the ends of the earth have seen your victory, we break forth in joyful song.

O for a thousand tongues to sing my great Redeemer's praise,
The glories of my God and king, the triumphs of his grace!

Today we seek joy—joy that cannot be taken away. May we hear your word and learn from you, Lord Jesus, that joy comes from obedience to your call to love as you have loved. That word stops us—obedience. We don't even like the sound of it. We have lived so long on the swampy ground of our own desires that the notion of rich and

solid ground on which we can plant our lives is a strange sugges-
tion—stranger yet when we hear that obedience is the fertile soil of
a firm ground. We deceive ourselves with comfortable lies that
enable us to take pleasure in ourselves and in the world. In a culture
that spends billions of dollars on self-indulgence, honors doing our
own thing, and defines success by money and toys, obedience is a
foreign language.

No wonder, Lord Jesus, that those who have discovered the deepest joy in their relationship with you have known that sloth, laziness,
and an uncaring nature is the essence of disobedience. Lack of care—
eat, drink, and be merry—and indifference to our well-being and the
welfare of others often escalate to destructive levels. Not to care for
oneself in a wholesome way and not to care for others leads from the
extremes of suicidal depression to giddy superficiality.

So you call us to obedience, to abide in your love (John 15:10). It
is in genuinely loving ourselves, seeking wholeness, and caring for
others in self-giving, sacrificial ways that we have a joy that is complete (v. 11). We seek that joy today.

As Christians we often feel like strangers in a foreign land, at battle with the world. Give us the grace to accept and the will to act on
the promise that those who conquer the world are those who believe
that Jesus is the Son of God (1 John 5:5). Enable us to know that
believing means obeying and obeying means loving (1 John 5:3). And
loving means caring for all, especially for the least of these. Give us
a sense of at-homeness in the world, though our obedience in love
makes us strangers. Make our yoke of obedience an easy burden by
giving us the joy that comes when we act not as servants, but as
friends (John 15:15). Grant that we may glorify you, O God, by giving ourselves to others through Jesus Christ our Lord, who reigns
with you in the Holy Spirit, one God, now and forever. Amen.

Seventh Sunday of Easter

Acts 1:15-17, 21-26   Psalm 1   1 John 5:9-13   John 15:6-19

Eternal Father, saving Christ, empowering Holy Spirit, ever one
God, we praise and worship you. You created life and called it good.

You could have created and abandoned us to our fate, but you didn't. You continue to create. You keep us alive and growing through Christ, the living water (John 4:11-14). It is by the stream of his living water that we would plant our lives. We know that it is only through his constant refreshing that we stay alive and bear fruit for your Kingdom (Psalm 1:3). Lord Jesus, we would be an answer to your prayer, your holy people dwelling in your grace and love for the sake of the world (John 17:17-19). Etch the truth indelibly on our minds, that others will believe only as they see reason to believe in us.

We remember your word, O God: The nations will realize that I am God when with their own eyes they can see my holiness through you (Ezekiel 36:23). We shudder at such a demanding call. We tremble at the thought that unless we are holy we will be of no use for you in the world. Teach us, Lord, how to be in the world but not of the world. Guide our wayward feet in the paths of righteousness (Psalm 1:1-2). Deliver us from the seduction of the broad way of "everyone else is doing it," "what difference can one person make?" "I'll try it just this once," and "after all, I deserve happiness." Give us backbone. We don't want to be like chaff the wind drives in every direction (Psalm 1:4).

Lord Jesus, we would be the answer to your prayer: as you are one with the Father, we would be one with you. Enable us to so abide in you and your love that we become like trees planted by the stream of your grace and bear the fruit that will inspire others to believe in you (Psalm 1:3; John 17:21).

Lord Jesus, we would be an answer to your prayer to shine forth the glory given you by the Father and given us by you (John 17:22). Let your glory be seen in the joy that is ours when we share your love with others (v. 13). Let your glory be seen as we make known your name (v. 26), the name that is above every name, the name sent by God (v. 25) to reveal himself as Savior, teacher, good shepherd, truth, light, comfort, healer, hope, and Lord. Lord Jesus, be glorified in us (v. 10). Call forth from our congregation those persons gifted for special ministry (Acts 1:24-25):

- teaching our children
- serving in our inner-city mission *[name specific areas of ministry]*
- being ministers of reconciliation among *[name ethnic groups or places of tension]*

Some may be called to places beyond our community, even to other lands. Give them the will to respond.

As by the Holy Spirit you gave to your apostles many excellent gifts, give your grace to all servants of your church. Empower us with diligence and faithfulness that we may fulfill our various ministries. Grant that we may follow where you lead and live in joyful obedience to your will. Replenish us with holiness of life. Fill us with the power of your Holy Spirit that by word, deed, and sign, we may serve you faithfully to the glory of your name and the building of your church. In your name, O God, made known to us in Jesus (John 17:6), we pray as he taught us, Our Father ...

Ascension Sunday

Directions: The Ascension of our Lord is one of the most undercelebrated events in the life of the church, and yet it is perhaps one of the most theologically significant. The clapping of hands is a frequent practice of the psalmist, signifying an expression of intense joy. Invite those who will to clap their hands three times following the words, "We clap our hands with cries of joy." Rehearse this several times prior to the prayer.

As an introduction to the prayer, invite the congregation to stand and read aloud with strong voice Psalm 47:1-6, printed either in the bulletin or on the screen.

Acts 1:1-11   Psalm 47   Ephesians 1:15-23   Luke 24:44-53

God of power and might, highly exalted, reigning over all nations (Psalm 47:7, 8), we clap our hands with cries of joy (v. 1). How awesome are you, O Lord, most high (v. 2). Not only did you raise your Son, Jesus, from the dead, but also you brought him to glory with you and seated him at your right hand, far above all rule and authority, power and dominion, and every name that is named not only in this age, but also in the age to come (Ephesians 1:20-21).

We clap our hands with cries of joy.

Jesus, once a baby in his mother's arms, is not that now. Jesus, once a carpenter, teacher, companion, and friend, walking the paths of the earth is not so now. Jesus, whose healing love mercifully blessed all he touched, all whom Jesus could see and hear and speak to, is not limited by time and space now. Jesus, a self-giving servant who hung on a cross, pouring out the blood of love on our behalf, is not hanging on the cross now. You raised him from the dead.

So we clap our hands with cries of joy.

But there is more. "God has ascended amid shouts of joy, the LORD amid the sounding of trumpets" (Psalm 47:5 NIV). So we sing praises to you our God and King (v. 6). You have brought your Son to you in glory. You have put everything under his feet and appointed him to be head of everything (Ephesians 1:22).

So we clap our hands with cries of joy.

We remember his teaching, his miracles, his compassionate care; we remember his death, the awful suffering, his body wracked with pain, but his spirit undaunted, his love undying—a substitute for our sin—we remember his resurrection, your mighty power exerted in him as you raised him from the dead (Ephesians 1:20).

So we clap our hands with cries of joy.

And today, we would especially remember his ascension. The curtain has gone up on a new act in your redemptive drama. The Spirit of this ascended one has been poured out on his followers and the church was born and is alive. You gave Jesus rule and authority and dominion, put all things under his feet *for* the church, *which is his body*, the fullness of him who fills all in all (Ephesians 1:22-23).

So we clap our hands with cries of joy.

So here we are as church today, your body, the dwelling place of the wonder of your presence. O Lord, how can we sit still? How can there be any hint of dullness in our worship? Let our praises soar; let the trumpets raise the roof.

O Lord, how can we sit still?

[Note: A drumroll or a few bars from the trumpet to be sounded here if possible or the choir might sing a triumphant chorus before the pastor/leader continues the prayer.]

We are your church, Lord, the dwelling place of wonder, *the wonder of your presence,* your presence making us a home of grace, a redemptive fellowship. As a home of grace we are a home for all. Through your Holy Spirit, confront us, Lord Jesus. Confront us with judgment that if we are not a home for all, we are not a home *at all.*

Confront us with judgment that if we are not a home for all, we are not a home at all.

We are your church, Lord, the dwelling place of wonder, *the wonder of the gospel.* We remember how you joined those on the road to Emmaus and opened their minds to understand the scriptures, to believe what all the prophets have declared (Luke 24:25), and to know you had to suffer to be our Savior (v. 26). We pray that our church will be a fellowship of teaching and learning, where the gospel is preserved and shared, where the faith once and for all delivered to the saints (Jude 3) is proclaimed, where hungry souls find bread not stones.

We are your church, O Lord, the dwelling place of wonder. *The wonder of the Holy Spirit's power.* We are here, waiting for "the promise of the Father" (Acts 1:4-5), the promise of power (Acts 1:8). Come, Holy Spirit:

be the fire in our hearts
be the wind in our sails
be the strength in our wills

that we may stay centered in Christ and be his witnesses in Jerusalem, Judea, Samaria, and the uttermost parts of the earth (Acts 1:8).

We are your church, O Lord, the dwelling place of wonder. We quiver with excitement. We are your body, and we want your presence and glory to pervade the whole creation. We will worship and serve you until the kingdoms of the world become your Kingdom and you shall reign forever and ever. Amen.

Praying with Posture

authenticates prayer ...

Joining nonverbal cues in harmony with spoken words.

(Some estimates indicate up to 95 percent of communication is nonverbal.)

Sitting before the Lord reveals

- an intimate intention to relate in conversation

- a contemplative presence before God

- the desire to inquire and listen.

Then King David went in and sat before the LORD,
and he said:
"Who am I, O Sovereign LORD, and what is my family,
that you have brought me this far?"

2 Samuel 7:18 NIV

Pentecost

Acts 2:1-21	Ezekiel 27:1-14	Psalm 104:24-35
	Romans 8:22-27	John 15:26-27; 16:4-15

We come to you today, O God, praising you for who you are:
God, the creator who gives us strength. How manifold are your
works; may your glory endure forever (Psalm 104:24-31).

God the redeemer, Jesus Christ, who saves us by his suffering love on the cross—the victorious power of the resurrection—and gives us peace.

God the sustainer, blessed Holy Spirit, who comforts, guides, and empowers.

We come today with full hearts, praising you for who you are and for all the marvelous things you have done (Psalm 104:24-30). If we were alone, we might be whistling or laughing, our feet barely touching the ground as we rehearse your mighty deeds and celebrate our life in the Spirit. Here in worship we pray, we sing with joy, and we open our hearts to hear your word. Come to us today, Spirit-giving God. As by your breath you gave life in first creation, then through your Son breathed new life into the disciples, now breathe new life into us.

Breathe new life into us.

Come as our advocate to convict us of our sins (John 16:8-11)—our sins of wrongdoing, injustice, and the violation of our bodies as the temples of your Holy Spirit; our sins in failing to act, failing to show mercy, and failing to speak out on your behalf and on behalf of the least of these; even our sins of pretension and presumption—pretending to be holy, presuming on your grace. In silence now, we confess our personal sins:

[Note: Offer at least one minute of complete silence before proceeding with the prayer.]

Come, Holy Spirit, to guide us into truth (John 16:13). We walk in darkness without your light. Even our thought patterns are poisoned by our sins of selfishness and the seduction of wealth and security. Bring us to the place where we are so humble in mind that we will think your thoughts after you. Be our sanctifier; purify our desires and motives, and consecrate our wills.

Blessed Holy Spirit, we know that your primary work is to glorify Christ through us (John 16:14). Our hearts dance when we retain the awareness that Jesus declares, "When the Spirit of truth comes, he willl guide you into all truth. He will not be presenting his own ideas; he will be telling you what he has heard. He will tell you about

---

the future. He will bring me glory by revealing to you whatever he receives from me" (John 16:13-14 NLT), and offers all that is his to us (1 Corinthians 3:21). By your power may we declare and offer his gift to others.

O Holy Spirit, pour out your aliveness and power on your people, the church. Enliven these dry bones (Ezekiel 37:6); put the flesh of love upon us that we may incarnate your presence (v. 8); breathe life into our structures, our relationships, our committees, our study classes, our prayer groups, our ministries, and our music and worship (vv. 9-10).

O Holy Spirit, by whose breath life rises vibrant out of death, come to create and renew the face of the earth (Psalm 104:30). Renew, inspire, kindle your fire in our hearts. Teach us to speak and to hear, to act and to wait, that all we are and do will be Spirit-shaped and Spirit-led.

Praise to you, God our Father. Praise to you, Christ, Son, and Savior. Praise to you, Holy Spirit—the same spirit who brooded over Creation, spoke through the prophets, was breathed on by the disciples after the resurrection, and was poured out and made available for all on the day of Pentecost—to whom be all honor and glory, both now and for all eternity. Amen.

Trinity Sunday

Isaiah 6:1-8   Psalm 29   Romans 8:12-17   John 3:1-17

Eternal God, Father, Son, Holy Spirit, we ascribe to you the glory due your name. We worship you in the splendor of your holiness (Psalm 29:2). We are overwhelmed with the thundering of your glory (v. 3).

God, as a loving, wise, present Father.

God as Savior, Jesus, taking upon himself the form of a servant and becoming obedient unto death on a cross (Philippians 2:6-8), thus putting to death our sin by the sacrifice of himself (Hebrews 9:26).

God as Holy Spirit, making Jesus known, enlivening, empowering, guiding, giving birth to, and sustaining the church.

So, we see you, Lord God, high and lifted up, and we cry, "Holy, holy, holy is the Lord Almighty; the whole earth is full of your glory" (Isaiah 6:3).

We confess that we have sinned and fallen short of your glory. It is becoming more real to us—that we are sinners in a world of sinners, persons of unclean lips among a people of unclean lips. We see you holy and we cry, "Woe is me" (Isaiah 6:5).

Like Nicodemus, we come to you for one thing but are surprised that what you give is not what we expected, but what we need. We need cleansing, new life. Though we know your grace and have accepted your forgiveness, our proneness to wander is strong, the grip of sin not completely severed. We need your Spirit. By the power of your Spirit, we put to death our sinful nature (Romans 8:12). We know enough to know that if we live according to our sinful nature, we will die; but if by the Spirit we put to death the misdeeds of the body, we will live (v. 13).

Like Nicodemus, we would come to you as teacher. Educate us. Give us a clear understanding of your will. Guide us in knowing where to go, how far to go, when to move, and when to stop. Bring to birth within us the new thing that will pervade our being and doing as your children, friends and co-laborers with Christ, living in the Spirit who raised Jesus from the dead (Romans 8:11).

Teach us compassion. Increase concern in us, especially concern for the poor. Though we are separated from them by position, power, and resources, enable us to preserve concern and care for them. In silence now we picture them in our minds and hold them in our hearts.

[Note: Offer a full minute of silence before continuing with the prayer.]

Teach us patience. How desperate is our need. How easily we become impatient with family members and close friends. How much more easily we become impatient with those about whom we're concerned. We even stop praying for those with whom we're impatient. Make us aware of how sinful this is. Give us enough patience at least to keep these persons in our prayers. In silence now we name these persons.

[Note: Offer a pause here for silent reflection.]

Teach us confidence and deliver us from fear.

Teach us confidence and deliver us from fear. We know that the dread of illness can be as damaging, and sometimes more damaging, than the illness itself. The fear of failure can be more fatal than the failure itself. We have so many faceless fears—fears that have no substance, no shape—that we can face and fight: fear of criticism, fear of the future, fear of old age; and yes, many of us here today are haunted in our sleepless nights with fear of death. O Lord, give us, deep within, the awareness of your nearness and loving concern, that we may be confident and fear no evil, for you are with me (Psalm 23:4).

As the shadow of a snake can't sting, so undergird us with consciousness of your presence that we will be delivered from fear of the many shadows that invade our minds and hearts. Give us the assurance that because we have received the spirit of Son-ship, we are no longer slaves to fear (Romans 8:15). The Spirit testifies with our spirit that we are God's children. So we cry, "Abba, Father!" *[pause]* "Jesus, Savior!" *[pause]* "Holy Spirit, life-giver" *[pause]*—"three in one, blessed Trinity. Amen."

Endnotes

1. We are indebted to Brian Rhea, a student and Chapel Intern at Asbury Theological Seminary, who crafted the body of this prayer for use in the season of Lent.

2. We are indebted to Brian Rhea, seminary student and worship intern, for portions of the body of this prayer, which was powerfully offered as part of our worship in the season of Lent.

Extraordinary Prayers for Ordinary Time

$\mathcal{I}$n the following section we offer a series of prayers for general use. We invite you to pray the story by adding to these prayers from the Psalms the content of other scriptures you plan to use in worship. In recognizing the common lot of humanity, these prayers capture both longing and lament while remembering the storied goodness of God amid celebration of God's glorious character.

Psalm 1

[Note: This prayer may be used effectively at a time of change or transition. To use it otherwise, please eliminate references in the prayer to transition.]

Ever-living, ever-faithful, ever-loving God, you are unchanging in your nature. There is no shadow of turning with you. As we begin this new year (as we come to this time of change and transition— *[name particular circumstance]*), we rejoice that you watch over the path of the just, you care for us, and we walk under your protection. You are willing to walk with us. More that that, your deep desire is to be with us always, to guide, to strengthen, to stir up and calm down. You've made the path plain. Joy comes to those who follow your leading; futility and destruction to those who disregard and resist your presence (Psalm 1:1, 4).

We confess that we do not delight in the law of the Lord; we do not meditate on your word day and night (Psalm 1:2). We are lazy in our Bible study, less than faithful in attending to spiritual disciplines. We go to the Bible when we need an answer to a problem or guidance in decision making. We don't live with your word, so it is not a lamp to our feet and a light to our path. Forgive us, Lord. Give us a new will to practice holy habits, to aspire for perfection, to cultivate virtues, to persevere in discipline. Make our pursuit of holiness of heart and life so sincere and dominant that we will know how dependent we are upon divine grace. Enable us to plant our feet firmly in your word and in a life of seeking prayer, that we will flourish spiritually like trees by fresh streams of water (Psalm 1:3), bearing fruit for your kingdom.

We commit ourselves anew to abide in you, loving Jesus. May your presence remind us daily of your forgiveness. Enable us to grow in your strength and in expressing your love. May your presence in us be so real that others will no longer see us, but see you, Lord Jesus.

Keep our eyes upon the needs and our ears sensitive to the pleading of others, fill our hearts with compassion, and strengthen our wills to act on your behalf for the sake of your kingdom. May we be cheered by your presence and move through these coming days without even a hint of anxiety, so that your peace may flow from our lives.

To you, God the Father, God the Son, and God the Holy Spirit, be all glory and honor now and forever more. Amen.

Psalm 2

Eternal God, what joy is ours today and always when we find our protection and refuge in you. These are unsettled times. Nations are raging around us. The powers of the earth plot against one another and against your kingdom reign (Psalm 2:1-2). The turmoil in _____, the threat of war in _____, the racial tension in our city, the anger that may erupt at any time—it seems as though there is a conspiracy against peace and justice.

Yet your word tells us that you laugh (Psalm 2:4) and that even in the midst of apparent darkness and chaos, we are to rejoice (v. 11). We know something about rejoicing. We sing our songs of joy, and we lift our voices in praise and thanksgiving. But you call us to rejoice with *trembling* (v. 11). We know little about trembling. Maybe we have missed something. Your word says you laugh at the foolishness and folly of those who act contrary to your will; it also says that you rebuke them in anger (v. 5) and that your anger may flare up in an instant (v. 11). So we had better tremble. We had better know that in your presence we are on holy ground.

Make that a part of our awareness—that you will not forever allow sin and wickedness to prevail and your will to be thwarted. Enable us in our rejoicing to be in trembling, so that we may order our lives according to your guidance and commands. Thus may we live in awe and reverence before you.

May we live in awe and reverence before you.

Eternal God, the one enthroned in heaven (Psalm 2:4), you have given us the privilege of prayer, the awesome opportunity of sharing with you. Through the psalmist you speak to us, "Ask of me, and I will make the nations your inheritance" (v. 8). How blessed we are. Unique in all creation, you have crowned us with glory and honor (Psalm 9:5), giving us the capacity to speak and listen to you. Why? Why, O Lord, do we squander such a breathtaking possibility?

You are sovereign over all creation. Yet you have made us partners in your kingdom enterprise, not only through our action, but also through our praying. Make real to us the awesome fact that there are some things God either cannot or will not do until and unless people pray. You have made our praying essential for your action. "If my people who are called by my name, will humble themselves and pray and seek my face and turn from their wicked ways, then will I hear from heaven and forgive their sin and will heal their land" (2 Chronicles 7:14 NIV).

We hear and respond for a season, but how easily we forget and forsake our resolution to pray. Forgive us. Do not forsake us and allow us to stand alone in our arrogant satisfaction, our self-serving pursuits, our superficial notions of self-sufficiency, the seductive pull of success and material security. Free us even from the desire for significance that is not fueled by compassion for others and a willingness to serve. Enable us to plant our feet firmly on the path of joyful obedience. May we find our happiness as we take refuge in you (Psalm 2:11). We join others who are walking in your way as we pray the prayer you taught us, Our Father . . .

Psalm 9:9-20

We come with hearts full of praise, O God, to you who is enthroned in glory forever. We give thanks to you with our whole being, our voices, our music, the movement of our bodies, the lifting of our heads, the clapping of our hands. May our sound and our silence exult in you (Psalm 9:1-2).

We come in confidence, for you, O Lord, have not forsaken those who seek you (Psalm 9:10). We come in consolation, knowing you are a stronghold for the oppressed (v. 9). We come as children to the arms of a loving parent because we know you do not forget the cries of the afflicted (v. 12).

We know you do not forget the cries of the afflicted.

We come in awe. We are not unlike the disciples when you rebuked the winds and brought a dead calm to the stormy sea (Mark 4:39). We are often stunned by your presence in our lives, the unexpected ways you act, and your refusal to fit into our perception of what is proper and rational.

Lord, will we forever be brainwashed by the media and even a superficial understanding of the Christian faith into thinking that life should be easy or painless or reasonable.

Will we ever learn that it is not easy or painless or reasonable to be a Christian?

How can we even think of ease or comfort when the center of our faith is the cross?

How can we be seduced by the call to be reasonable and rational when you, the One who created all the galaxies and movement of the stars in their courses, gave ultimate expression to your power in the powerlessness of a little baby?

How long will we be intimidated by those who demand rational convincing when the core of our faith is that the ordinary baby of Bethlehem grew into a man who was fully human and simultaneously fully divine.

Teach us to understand faith more fully—beyond mere facts, transcending sight. For the unbelieving world, seeing is believing; but for us, believing is seeing: born of the Virgin Mary, made the blind see and the lame walk, healed lepers, embraced prostitutes and tax collectors, suffered under Pontius Pilate, was crucified, was dead and buried, and on the third day arose. Lead us into a faith in which believing becomes seeing.

May we see you more clearly, love you more dearly, and follow you more nearly day by day. This much we know:

that to yield to you is to be made and kept whole *[pause]*
that to be bent by your discipline is to become straight *[pause]*
that to be empty of self-seeking is to be full *[pause]*
that to be exhausted and worn out in compassionate-loving service is to be renewed. *[pause]*

Loving Father, make us people of one heartbeat as we rejoice in your salvation and recount all your praises and pray the prayer Jesus taught to us when he said, Our Father . . .

Psalms 9 and 30

We come to you today, O God, with full hearts, praising you for who you are—creator, redeemer, Lord—and thanking you for all the marvelous things you have done. If we were alone, we might be whistling, laughing, walking with a lightness in our steps. Here together we pray; we sing with joy and open our hearts to hear your word.

Praying together, we remember that you are a shelter for the oppressed, a safe harbor for the suffering, a refuge, a stronghold for those who are troubled. In silence now we name those we know who are physically ill; estranged from spouses, parents, and children; and financially burdened or without work.

[Insert other concerns from the people at this point.]

Ever-aware, everlasting God, who hears our laughter and our cry, we wait in your presence, claiming the promise that though tears fill our nights, joy comes in the morning (Psalm 30:5). For some of us, the night is not marked by twelve hours of darkness, but by a son who is involved in a blazing drug addiction, by a daughter who has just become a single parent because her uncaring husband has gone his selfish way, by a parent who doesn't recognize her children because her memory no longer provides knowledge, by the loan company that is threatening foreclosure, by the word coming out that our position is being phased out, and we have two more months of work.

We walk a tear-salted path and we wonder if the dawn will ever come. But we cling to hope because we trust you. We know you care and we know you listen—so we simply lift our hearts to you. With your divine stethoscope, hear our hearts beating and let us know that you love us. Kindle in us confidence as you give ear to our words, O Lord, and as you listen to our sighs.

We long to know you so well, and want those for whom we pray to be in such close relationship with you, that we will trust you completely and know that you will not ignore us when we cry for help (Psalm 9:10).

You have promised that the needy will not always be forgotten and that hope for the poor will be rekindled (Psalm 9:18). Use us as individuals and as a congregation as channels through which your promise is fulfilled.

Use us as individuals and as a congregation as channels through which your promises are fulfilled.

Increase in us the confidence that you are sovereign, Lord, and that you will reign forever. Even though we tremble in the knowledge that you judge with justice and rule with fairness (Psalm 9:8), we place ourselves, our congregation, our community, and our nation before your throne.

We acknowledge that you are God and that we are merely human; and to defy you in any way is death, and to love and serve you is life. So, have mercy on us, that we may always rejoice in you. Hear us as we pray the prayer Jesus taught us, saying, Our Father . . .

Psalm 18

Directions: As a preparation for prayer, invite the congregation to read together Psalm 18:2-3. Print the text in the bulletin or on the screen.

The Lord is my rock, my fortress, and my deliverer, my God, my rock in whom I take refuge, my shield, and the horn of my salvation, my stronghold. I call upon the Lord, who is worthy to be praised, so I shall be saved from my enemies (Psalm 18:2-3).

Eternal God, we bless you as the rock of our salvation, our safe harbor in a time of storm. So lead us, lead us to "the rock that is higher than I." Be a shelter in the time of storm.

We trust you, O Lord, but confess that our trust is being tested. The forces of evil seem to have the upper hand. *[Name concerns such as these: in the Sudan today, twenty thousand more Christians were slaughtered, and in northern Nigeria, seven churches were burned and 682 Christians killed. Iraq continues to be a powder keg and the days slowly fold on one another with grave clothes wrapped around two or three, sometimes twelve or twenty more persons.]* More is at stake here than the prevailing of one political understanding over another or the dominance of a narrowly defined religious expression. At stake are the lives of little children; the hope of life, liberty, and the pursuit of happiness; the promise of security and peace; the opportunity for creative expression; but perhaps more immediate, food and shelter.

Eternal God of the covenant, you have not turned away from your people but are faithful even in the face of our rejection. Your steadfast love endures forever (Psalm 118:1). We confess our unfaithfulness and our failure to trust you. We have trusted in ourselves, our wealth, our abilities, and our political and social contacts. As a nation, we have trusted in our economic systems, our military might, our technological know-how. We repent. Though we're not here in sackcloth and ashes, we are full of shame, and our hearts are heavy. We feel the burden of our distorted self-trust and our failure to trust you.

It is confusing and frustrating. Our trust is being tested. But here in this place at this time, we reaffirm our faith in you, and we listen to your word to give us an ongoing adjustment in our thinking and also a clear call to wholeness, to the Kingdom activity you intend for us in the days ahead. May even the small duties of our day shine with the beauty of your countenance. May we believe that inevitably the glory of your presence will shine in the common tasks of every day.

We affirm with confidence, "The LORD lives! Blessed be my rock, and exalted be the God of my salvation" (Psalm 18:46). O God, we pray for our church today. We want to be a kingdom presence in this community, an entryway for pilgrims seeking your presence and power. So, our Father, make the door of this house "wide enough to receive all who need human love and fellowship, narrow enough to shut out all envy, pride, and strife. Make its threshold smooth enough to be no stumbling block to children, nor to straying feet, but rugged and strong enough to turn back the tempter's power. God, make the door of this house the gateway to thine eternal kingdom" (Prayer on the door of St. Stephen's Church in London).

Hear us as we pray the prayer Jesus taught us, saying, Our Father . . .

Psalm 27

We lift our eyes to you, O Lord, to you who are enthroned in the heavens. We lift our voices to you, Lord Jesus Christ, to you who suffered for us, stretching out your arms on the cross for the whole world.

We pray with the psalmist, "The LORD is my light and my salvation; whom shall I fear?" (Psalm 27:1). Yet honestly, we confess we are afraid. Our lives are gripped by the fear of terror. We brood over the possible loss of loved ones. If we are honest before you, Lord, we must confess that fear is the most pervasive reality we feel. And yet we boldly declare with the psalmist, "The LORD is the stronghold of my life; of whom shall I be afraid? When evildoers assail me to devour my flesh—my adversaries and foes—they shall stumble and fall. Though an army encamp against me, my heart shall not fear; though war rise up against me, yet I will be confident" (vv. 1-3).

Teach us your ways, Lord, that we may walk in these your paths; that our fear might give way to faith and hope and love.

"One thing I asked of the LORD, that will I seek after: to live in the house of the LORD all the days of my life, to behold the beauty of the LORD, and to inquire in his temple. For he will hide me in his shelter in the day of trouble; he will conceal me under the cover of his tent; he will set me high on a rock. Now my head is lifted up above my enemies all around me" (Psalm 27:4-6*a*).

And though our enemies do evil, forgive us for demonizing them. Come, Holy Spirit, and teach us the way we do not know and are reluctant to go. Teach us to pray for them. We long for a day when you will beat swords into plowshares (Micah 4:3) and the lion will lie down with the lamb.

With the psalmist we affirm, we believe that we shall see the goodness of the Lord in the land of the living. Wait for the Lord; be strong, and let your heart take courage; wait for the Lord (Psalm 27:13-14). So here in silence we wait on you. *[Offer a full minute of silence.]*

Hear us as we pray the prayer Jesus taught us, saying, Our Father . . .

Psalm 104

Praise the Lord, O my soul. Bless your holy name. You are great, O Lord our God. You are clothed with splendor and majesty (Psalm 104:2). The entire cosmos—the wind and the water, the mountains and the valleys, the birds and the bees and the beasts, night and day, moon and stars—is the work of your hands. You have bound it all together: springs, to give water to quench even the thirst of wild donkeys (v. 11); trees, to bear fruit, and also to provide nests for the birds that they may bless us with their songs; grass and plants for the cattle; "and wine to gladden the human heart, oil to make the face shine, and bread to strengthen the human heart. The trees of the LORD are watered abundantly" (vv. 15-16).

Praise the Lord, O my soul. Bless your holy name. As you moved over the watery chaos and brought the cosmos and its creatures into existence, you created humans in your image, breathed into us not only life, but *your* life. We celebrate our part in your created order. We confess that we have not been good stewards of this good earth you gave us dominion over. Not only have we wasted and ravished your creation here in our developed world, but also we have failed to use the resources that are ours to help cultivate the resources of underdeveloped sections of the world. The greatest sign of this is found in countless children living in distress throughout the world.

We remember millions of orphans on the continent of Africa dying of AIDS, of starvation, and of lack of clean water. *[Insert other current scenarios of need both locally and throughout the world.]* Forgive us, Lord.

Forgive us for quenching your divine spirit within us. Forgive us for defining ourselves by our fleshly passions, our biological drives. Forgive us for seeking a sense of worth in our appearance, our possessions, what we have achieved, the academic degrees, and the titles that have been bestowed upon us and the positions we hold. Invade our arrogant, self-centered worlds that are so cluttered with stuff—with material and external signs of our pride and superficial security. Confront our arrogance with your questions to Job:

Where were you when I laid the foundations of the earth? What supports its foundations, and who laid its cornerstone as the morning stars sang together and all the angels shouted for joy? Who defined the boundaries of the sea as it burst from the womb? Have you ever commanded the morning to appear and caused the dawn to rise in the East? Can you shout to the clouds and make it rain? Can you make lightning appear and cause it to strike as you direct it? Who gives intuition and instinct? Who is wise enough to count all the clouds? Who can tilt the water jars of heaven, turning the dry dust to clumps of mud? Who provides food for the ravens when their young cry out to God as they wander about in hunger (Job 38:4-7, 12; 34:38, 41)?

Forgive us, Lord. Forgive us for seeking first place, or positions of power and honor, for an unwillingness to drink the cup of obedience and suffering for the sake of your kingdom. Keep ever fresh in our minds the pattern of Jesus, your Son, our Savior and Lord, whose prayers you heard when he was human like us because of his reverent submission (Hebrews 5:7). Although he was your Son, he learned obedience from what he suffered (v. 8), an obedience that climaxed with his suffering on the cross.

Don't let us forget that he is our salvation as we seek to obey him, as he became our salvation by obeying you (Hebrews 5:9). Keep vividly in our minds the picture of him who was led like a lamb to the slaughter (Isaiah 53:7) in order to take our infirmities and carry our sorrows (v. 4) and was cursed for our iniquities to heal and bring us peace (v. 5).

And don't let us forget that this suffering and death was not an arbitrary substitute for our sins, but was to defeat all the forces that would enslave us, *[pause]* to renew your covenant and redeem us, *[pause]* ruling God, to renew your creation *[pause]*. So we join the morning stars and all your creation, singing, bless the Lord, O my soul, and all that is within me. Bless his holy name. Amen.

Psalm 139

Ever-present, ever-seeing, ever-listening, ever-loving God, you have searched us and know us. You know when we sit down and when we rise up; you discern our thoughts from faraway. You search out our path and our lying down and are acquainted with all our ways (Psalm 139:1-3). We do not have to invite you to be present with us; you are always present. Our deepest prayer today is for an awareness of your presence.

When the dawn appears, when the morning light grows, when midday burns, when the shadows fall, and when clear night and deep darkness come, may we know you are with us.

Let no words cross our lips that are not your words, for we know even before a word is on our tongues, you know it completely (Psalm 139:4).

Let no thoughts that are not your thoughts linger in our minds, for we know how weighty your thoughts are, how vast the sum of them is (Psalm 139:17).

Let no deeds be done by any one of us that are not your deeds, for we know very well how wonderful are your works (Psalm 139:14).

Lord, forgive our pride of self-will; sever from each of us the binding chains of always having to be in control. Teach us to know with the psalmist how futile it is: "If I say, 'Surely the darkness shall cover me, and the light around me become night,' even the darkness is not dark to you; the night is as bright as the day, for darkness is as light to you" (Psalm 139:11-12). We look for light but find darkness, for brightness but walk in gloom. We grope like those who have no eyes, we stumble at noon as in twilight.

You are creator and we praise you, for we are fearfully and wonderfully made (Psalm 139:14). You are our ever-seeking, ever-saving Redeemer. Your loving hands are always upon us (v. 5), molding, transforming our present stature even as you formed us in our mothers' wombs. You are life-giving Spirit, present, and giving hope even in the hells of our life (v. 8).

[Note: Offer special intercession for those in "hellish circumstances"—for example, those whose teenage child was killed in an accident, those suffering an incurable disease, the single mom whose selfish husband left her, those who are living during famine and war.]

So, here we are, Lord. Search us and know our hearts: test us and know our thoughts. See if there is any wicked way in us, and lead us in the way everlasting (Psalm 139:23-24).

Blessed be your name forever. You are light and in you is no darkness at all (1 John 1:5). To us you sent your Son, the light of the world, through whom our darkness is passing away. We praise him, with you and the Holy Spirit, forever and ever. Amen.

You are light and in you is no darkness at all.

Benediction

May you have peace within today.
May you trust God that you are exactly where you are meant to be.
May you use those gifts that you have received, and pass on the love
that has been given to you.
May you be content knowing you are a child of God.
Let this presence settle into your bones and allow your soul the free-
dom to sing, dance, praise, and love.
It is there for each and every one of you who choose to claim it.

Prayer of Saint Thérèse de Lisieux (1873–1897)